HOW TO BE HUMAN IN AN INHUMAN WORLD

COLOSSIANS FOR DAILY LIVING

Robert C. Beasley

An Imprint of Sulis International Press
Los Angeles | Dallas | London

Cover graphic by gremlin (iStock/Getty Images).
Cover design by Sulis International Press.

ISBN (print): 978-1-958139-41-7
ISBN (eBook): 978-1-958139-42-4

Published by Keledei Publications
An Imprint of Sulis International
Los Angeles | Dallas | London

www.sulisinternational.com

Contents

To Stacy, my partner in life, who constantly shows me the fierce loyalty of the love of God.

HOW TO BE HUMAN IN AN INHUMAN WORLD

The way we live is killing us. It is killing us because we were not made to live this way.

Literally, it is killing us. For the first time since the end of World War I, life expectancy in the United States declined in 2017 and has declined every year since.[1] Why? The main reasons are suicide, drug overdose, and alcohol related deaths. Why is this happening when the United States is the richest nation in the world? As sociologists Case and Deaton explain, "All the deaths show great unhappiness with life, either momentary or prolonged. It is tempting to classify them all as suicides, done either quickly with a gun or by standing on and kicking away a chair with a rope around the neck, or slowly with drugs and alcohol."[2] Medical professionals rightly warn that we are experiencing a mental health crisis, marked by anxiety, depression, addiction, and loneliness. The way we live is making us sick.

---

[1]See Lenny Bernstein, "U.S. Life Expectancy Declines Again, a Dismal Trend Not Seen Since World War I," *Washington Post*, November 29, 2018.

[2]Quoted in Alain Ehrenberg, *The Weariness of the Self: Diagnosing the History of Depression in the Contemporary Age* (Montreal & Kingston: McGill-Queen's University Press, 2010), 38-39.

What is it about the way we live that is making us so sick? There are many factors contributing to our malady, but let me mention a few:

- ***Stress.*** Technology has rapidly accelerated the pace of our lives, increasing our daily stress levels.
- ***Constant Information Flow:*** Technology has allowed us to receive horrible news from all over the world constantly, something our bodies and minds are not designed to handle.
- ***Social media***. Numerous studies have shown that heavy social media use leads to depression, anxiety, loneliness, and even suicidal thoughts.[3]
- ***Political polarization***. Political compromise for the good of our country and faith in government is a thing of the past, resulting in divisiveness and anger.
- ***Racial tension.*** COVID-19 made us realize that we have not resolved racial prejudice and tension.
- ***Artificial Intelligence***. Will AI provide great breakthroughs in science and medicine, or is it the existential threat that even its creators and experts fear?
- ***Climate Change.*** Lack of community. 24-7 Work. Lack of meaning and purpose. Lack of free speech and fear of being "cancelled." China, Russia, Ukraine, Israel/Hamas, Iran, lack of leadership, the threat of nuclear war. Inflation and the uncertainties in a global economy.

---

[3]See, for example, Berryman C., Ferguson C., Negy C. *Psychiatric Quarterly*. 2018; 89:307-314; Coyne SM, Rogers AA, Zurcher JD, Stockdale L, Booth M. *Computers and Human Behavior*. 2020; 104: 106-160.

Is it any wonder that we are having a mental health crisis, with skyrocketing anxiety and depression?

Is this how humans are supposed to live? Our minds and bodies shout, "No!" The reason our way of life is killing us is because the way we live is *dehumanizing.* Our minds, bodies, and our emotions were not made to live like this. As Alan Noble writes in *You Are Not Your Own: Belonging to God in an Inhuman World:*

> A defining feature of life in the modern West is our awareness of society's inhumanity and our inability to imagine a way out of it. This inhumanity includes everything from abortions, mass shootings, and widespread coverups of sexual abuse to meaningless jobs, broken communities, and TV shows that are only good for numbing our anxiety for thirty minutes. We weren't made to live like this, and most of us know it. But either we don't care, or we don't think we can do anything about it. So, the mode that best describes our day-to-day experience is 'survival.'[4]

If the diagnosis is that we are sick, then we need to ask some questions:

- What does it mean to be human?
- What is it about our way of life that is making us so sick?
- What do we humans need to become "healthy" again, to become *human* again?

---

[4]Alan Noble, *You Are Not Your Own: Belonging to God in an Inhuman World* (Downers Grove, Il.: IVP, 2021), 1.

What Does it Mean to Be Human?

In 1954, psychologist Abraham Maslow articulated his "Hierarchy of Needs," a pyramid of basic needs that humans need to *flourish* or thrive, to have full or fruitful lives (see Maslow's pyramid below).[5] Maslow's hierarchy of needs is a good place to start as we consider what it means to be human.

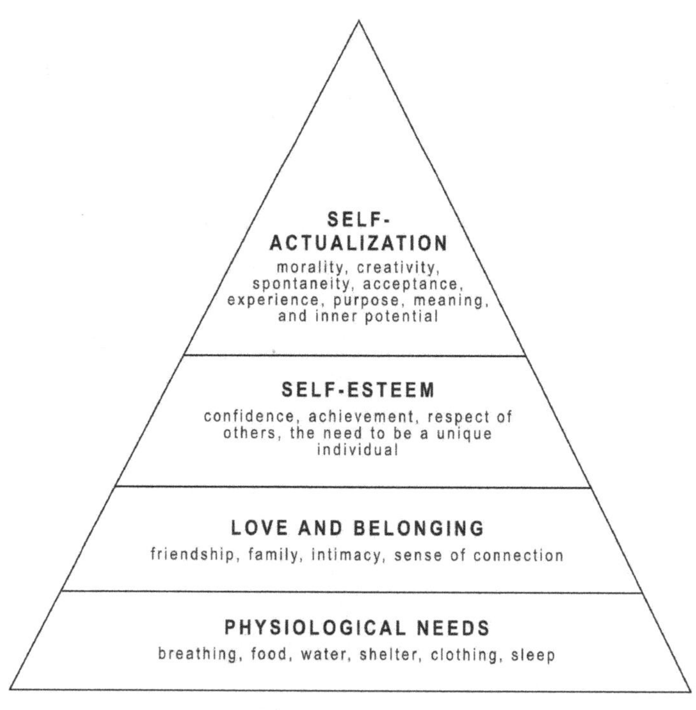

[5]Abraham Maslow, *Motivation and Personality* (New York: Harper and Row, 1954).

The first level is basic: food, water, shelter, clothing, and sleep. Although tragically, there are many in the U.S. who do not have these basic daily needs, most of us do. But what about that last one: *sleep*? The AMA suggests every person requires 7–9 hours of sleep a night. Are you getting that? Why not? Is it because you are stressed, anxious, or overworked? Maybe watching too much Netflix to distract you from the numbness of reality? At this basic level, we might say that t*o be human is to be rested and have a sense of peace and well-being.*

As we move up the ladder, we realize that we are not just physical creatures, we are social creatures. It turns out that to be human is to be *with* other people. Not just chatting online or texting; we need physical, human contact. Yet, our technological world has deepened our isolation and loneliness. Humans need community, and we cannot thrive without it. *To be human is to be in community. We want to belong.*

We need not just human interaction, we need deep levels of interaction. Studies have shown the absence of close relationships poses a more serious health risk than smoking, obesity, or lack of exercise.[6] We need friendship, family, intimacy, bonding, a sense of connection, love. And such love inevitably will require forgiveness because to be human also means to make mistakes. *To be human means to be loved.*

The fourth level goes even deeper: confidence, achievement, respect, the need to be a unique individual. From our earliest childhood, each of us have asked the question: "Who am I?" Each of us wants to "find our place in the world," to matter. *To be human means to have our identity affirmed and for our lives to matter.*

---

[6]See Paula R. Pietromonaco and Nancy L. Collins, "Interpersonal Mechanism Linking Close Relationships to Health," *American Psychologist* 72 (2017), 532-42.

The final level is what Maslow called "self-actualization," and it is a need deep within us as humans: meaning, purpose, morality, creativity—to become the most we can be. It turns out that we as humans can't live without meaning. And not just some abstract meaning; we want to be daily involved in something meaningful. Sociologist Jonathan Haidt, in his book *The Righteous Mind*, notes that "an obsession with righteousness (leading inevitably to self-righteousness) is the normal human condition."[7] Bringing together these notions of meaning, purpose, creativity, and "righteousness" is the concept of "Transcendence." Philosopher Charles Taylor notes that the lack of meaning and transcendence is at the heart of so many of our current cultural problems: "Running through all these attacks [on humanity] is the specter of meaninglessness: that as a result of the denial of transcendence, of heroism, of deep feeling, we are left with a view of human life which is empty, cannot inspire commitment, offers nothing really worthwhile, cannot answer the craving for goals we can dedicate ourselves to."[8] *To be human is to have meaning, purpose, transcendence, and hope*.

How Are We Missing the Mark?

What is it about our way of life that is depriving us of each of these, and why are we missing the mark of becoming fully human? It isn't for lack of trying. In fact, we are wearing ourselves out with every technique and drug available to find satisfaction and fullness. So why are we missing the mark?

---

[7]Jonathan Haidt, *The Righteous Mind: Why Good People are Divided by Politics and Religion* (New York: Vintage Books, 2012), xix.
[8]Charles Taylor, *A Secular Age* (Cambridge, MA: Belknap Press, 2007), 717.

Maybe one reason our world is dehumanizing is because we are going about it all wrong. Our world is constantly telling us stories of how to be a human, *and the basic assumption of these stories is that each of us decides in our own ways what it means to be a human.* It is like being given a car to drive and each of us gets to decide whether it is a car, a giraffe, or a horse. We also get to decide what sort of fuel to put in the tank. But cars are made a certain way, and so are humans. We need somebody who really knows what a human is supposed to be to tell us: *this is how to become human again.*

As Alan Noble points out, our secular society starts with the basic assumption that each of us can decide what it means to be human. This way of thinking is relatively recent in the history of humanity, arising only over the last 300 years and growing out of Enlightenment thinking. While there is freedom in this perspective (and freedom is a good thing), it also means we are each *responsible* for deciding everything about our lives. Noble calls this the "Responsibilities of Self-Belonging:" "the responsibility to justify our existence, to create an identity, to discover meaning, to choose values, and to belong."[9]

So, how have we fared in being responsible for our self-belonging? Have we become more human? Noble notes ways that society has helped us "become our own." But often, society's answers have contributed to our dehumanization. Noble gives us a good glimpse of our current cultural situation:

We Can Choose Our Own Identity. The defining value of our modern society is for each of us to be "our own person," to be true to the way we feel. We live in what sociologists call a "liquid" or "plastic" world, molding our identities to how we feel at any particular time. "Today, the self is entirely plastic, and the external world—right down to our bodies—is liquid,

[9]Noble, 35.

something that offers no firm ground upon which to build an identity."[10] We don't just want to be our own persons; we want (and naturally need) others to affirm who we are. Sociologists call this "expressive individualism," and it is the prevailing philosophy of our time: "we want everyone to recognize and affirm our identity precisely as we define that identity at this moment in time. And in order to get people to see me, I need to express myself—a lot."[11] Social media and technology help fuel this way of thinking. As Noble notes, "modern life feels like billions of people in the same room shouting their own name so that everyone else knows they exist and who they are —which is a fairly accurate description of social media."[12]

We Can Justify Our Existence. To justify our existence, we also need to be part of a worthy cause. And our world is filled with worthy causes: "We throw ourselves into the cause of the month, raise funds for this famine, petition the government to intervene in that grisly civil war; and then forget all about it next month when it drops off the CNN screen."[13] This often results in "good cause fatigue" and also leads to struggles for power. If each of us decides what is "right," then "'morality' turns out to be the assertion of someone's will upon someone else—an exercise of power, not truth."[14] Or, as Carl R. Trueman notes, "Human selves exist in dialogue with the terms of recognition set by the wider world. When that world is liquid, those terms are set by the loudest voices and the most dominant narratives."[15]

---

[10]Carl R. Trueman, *Strange New World: How Thinkers and Activists Redefined Identity and Sparked the Sexual Revolution* (Wheaton, Il: Crossway, 2022), 126.
[11]Noble, 25.
[12]Id.
[13]Taylor, 696.
[14]Noble, 29.
[15]Trueman, 127.

We Have the Politics. Politics is the preferred path to achieve affirmation of our identities, as well as to gain control and power. Politics has become "identity politics," or the organizing of political groups based on religion, race, ethnicity, gender, sexuality, or cultural preferences. Identity politics dominates our political process, so much so that things rarely get accomplished in Washington.

We Have the Technology. Advances in technology have also contributed to our ability to actually choose the persons we want to be, including curated social media posts, hormone injections, plastic surgery, and gender-transitioning procedures. New technologies and techniques are coming at us daily with ways to make us "happier." And technology is constantly driving us toward one of the greatest values of modern life: *efficiency*. We are barraged with notifications and technologies to become more efficient, more competitive. But efficiency is for machines, not for humans, and this constant drive toward efficiency is dehumanizing us.

The Pursuit of Happiness. If there is one central theme to our modern way of living, it is that all modern life is arranged around our "pursuit of happiness." Self is at the center of modern life, and we do everything we can to achieve happiness. A symbol and reflection of our elevation of the pursuit of happiness is *pornography.* No wonder pornography is one of the largest industries in the world--our way of life is pornographic in so many ways. As Noble writes:

> Pornography assumes that we are each our own and belong to ourselves. It's a tool that promises to give us a kind of personal validation, a sense of identity, a taste of meaningfulness, and a glimpse of intimate belonging. But by its own logic, pornography, like modernity, is an empty promise. Rather than helping us meet our

> responsibilities and cope with an inhuman world, it exacerbates our condition. Rather than bringing us closer to our humanity, it dehumanizes at every turn, turning our intimacy into instrumentality and leaving us addicted, depressed, exhausted, lonely, and bored—which also happens to be an accurate description of our society in general.[16]

While society promises happiness and self-actualization, its answers have made us *less human*. Its answers create new problems: "technique (porn as a tool for sexual validation and belonging) is used to cope with a problem (lack of intimacy and belonging) created by a technique (antidepressants) to cope with a problem (depression and anxiety) which grew out of the inhuman conditions of modern life."[17]

How Can We Become Human Again?

Our world is chaotic and dehumanizing. But we have been here before. Ancient Roman culture was in many ways like ours today. While the rich viciously pursued their own happiness, Roman cities were crime-infested, marked by infanticide, slavery, prejudice, inequality, and neglect of the poor. Roman culture was dehumanizing. But when you think about it, every generation has had its own dehumanizing ways. That, too, is a part of our humanity. *To be human also means to be broken.* We are all broken people living in a broken world. Is there anyone who can put us back together again?

Amid the inhumanity of the Roman Empire, there arose a message of hope, a message that rang true to our deepest needs

[16]Noble, 63-64.
[17]Noble, 68.

as humans, a message that "fit us" as humans. This message healed our brokenness and taught humans how to become human again. And the message originated with a *human, one human unlike any other human.* This human lived a life that was singularly unique in human history. Here is his "resume," if you will:

- He was born very poor and grew up in a backwater village.
- Although he was an ethnic minority, he was known for regularly associating with people from all racial and ethnic backgrounds.
- In a patriarchal world, he deliberately worked to elevate the status of women (and succeeded).
- His teaching has been described as the pinnacle of ethical thinking. But instead of giving us techniques to satisfy our selfish needs and pursue happiness, he said that the way to find ourselves is to "die" to our selfishness and live for others. He asked a haunting question that our world today still can't answer: "What good is it to gain the whole world but lose your soul?"
- He said that there really is a God, and he showed us how shockingly near and loving God is: like a Father who sees into our secret hearts, who cares for the weak and marginalized, and who pursues the heart of every human being the world over.
- He initiated what he called a new "kingdom," marked not by power, money, violence, fame, or the pursuit of happiness, but marked by humility, sacrifice, forgiveness, reconciliation, friendship, and love.
- He even started a new society where these character traits of love and forgiveness prevail, a safe place where humans

can learn to love across all boundaries, a place where humans can flourish. This society is now the largest single society in the world, as well as the greatest social revolution in human history.

- He was not afraid to fight against the power structures that oppressed humans, ultimately sacrificing his own life on behalf of others.

- Unlike politicians, he meant what he said about sacrificial love. Instead of fighting to save his neck, he willingly submitted to a public lynching, the worst type of execution possible. He let his hands and feet be nailed to a tree, hanging humiliated and naked for hours until he slowly died from asphyxiation and loss of blood. He said he was doing this for every human, exhausting and overcoming the powers that oppress us. He claimed that this sacrifice was from God himself, intended to reconcile us to God and to each other.

- Like every person that was crucified, he died. He was dead for two days. But on the third day, his mutilated body was transformed into a new *human*, with an indestructible body. But he wasn't some ephemeral spirit; *he was still a human with a human body, but one that will never die again.*

- Before ascending to heaven *with this human body*, he said, "All authority in heaven and on earth has been given to me." He promised to be with his followers always, and that where two or more of them came together, he would be with them. He promised that if we remain "in him" and allow him to "remain in us," we can actually become human again, for the first (and lasting) time.

I'm sure you have guessed who I am talking about: Jesus of Nazareth, whom Christians claim to be the one God of the universe, the Creator in the flesh. But for just a minute, let it sink in how *human* Jesus was and how that now, in heaven, Jesus still bears the marks of our *humanity*. We often think of God as "something up there where humans are not." But that kind of God has nothing to do with either the God of the Old Testament, and certainly not the God revealed in Jesus. We often forget that *the core message of Christianity is God stooping to raise us up as humans*, to not only dignify us as humans but to exalt us as humans with and in Jesus, the "Son of Man." In Jesus, God himself can show us how to become human again.

The Mind-Boggling Way to Become Human Again

The claims of Christianity are mind-boggling, but they are exactly what we as humans need to become human again, and especially in our modern world that has forgotten what it means to be human. If you haven't done so in a while, consider these core, yet profound, claims of the early Christians:

- No one has ever seen God, but Jesus has made God fully known.
- Jesus is the exact representation of God—everything we need to know about God is fully revealed in Jesus. Jesus is the image, or tangible presence, of the invisible God.
- Jesus is the reason everything exists; he is what the Greeks called the "Logos" ("Reason"). Jesus is the Reason there is a universe in the first place.
- Everything was created *by this Jesus—everything!* And not only created by this Jesus, but created *for Jesus*: to display the incredible love of God for humans through this Jesus.

- Jesus is the prototype, or *blueprint*, for humanity; Jesus is what humans are supposed to become.
- All the fullness of God was embodied in Jesus, and in Jesus humans can also have the "fullness" of everything that is good, true, joyful, peace-giving, loving.
- Jesus' horrible death was the place where the worst of evil exhausted all its power forever. All the "powers" of accusation, fear, shame, hate, alienation, and death were completely exhausted on Jesus, and now they have no power over us. Jesus frees us from all oppression to become all he created us to be.
- Jesus is the first human to overcome death, but most assuredly not the last. He is the portal of love through which humans might also live forever.
- Jesus provides the "sphere," the "safe place," where humans can become human again.
- Humans come together in this "safe place" as a community, and it is through being in this community that the Spirit of Jesus comes into our hearts, minds, and emotions and trains us to live life fully alive—to become human again.

These claims are sprinkled throughout the New Testament. But we find them most emphatically in a few places: the Gospel of John, the letter to the Hebrews, and most particularly from a short, power-packed letter that Paul and Timothy wrote to a young church in the town of Colossae, located in present day Turkey—the *letter to the Colossians.*

Colossians: A Pamphlet for Our Times

The apostle Paul wrote 13 letters that have been preserved for us (six of which he wrote with our co-author, Timothy). Out of all of these letters, I think there are two which speak especially to our world in the 21st century: *Colossians and Ephesians*. Why these two letters? Because both address the dehumanizing nature of a world without God, and both proclaim boldly that Jesus is the only way to restore our humanity. Both also stress that despite the power of the Roman Empire, Jesus is the true King and Emperor. Both letters also proclaim that Jesus is in charge, and that applies not only to the Roman Empire, but to all "powers" that seek control over our lives in one way or another. Jesus is in charge, not the Republicans or Democrats; not Google, Facebook, or Amazon; not China or Russia; not any "woke" philosophy on the one hand nor any ultra-conservative philosophy on the other. Jesus' crucifixion and resurrection unmasked, disarmed, and rendered powerless the Roman Empire and all the dehumanizing forces of the first century and every century, allowing humans to become human again.

Colossians and Ephesians are very similar; Colossians reads like a first draft of Ephesians, with Ephesians filling in and explicating the outline of similar themes found in Colossians. Read them together over a period of months, alternating one with the other, and your outlook on everything will be changed.

As you let these words, images, and ideas from Colossians and Ephesians "take root" and "dwell" in you, you will come to experience that the way of Jesus is the way to the most satisfying and flourishing life. Jesus makes us human again. As Tim Keller pointed out, the Jesus way of life provides:

- A meaning in life that suffering can't take away, but can even deepen.

- A satisfaction that isn't based on circumstances.
- A freedom that doesn't reduce community and relationships to thin transactions.
- An identity that isn't fragile or based on our performance or the exclusion of others.
- A way to both deal with guilt and forgive others without residual bitterness or shame.
- A basis for seeking justice that does not turn us into oppressors ourselves.
- A way to face not only the future, but death itself with poise and peace.
- An explanation for the senses of transcendent beauty and love we often experience.[18]

God loves humans. God loved us so much, he became a human. He loved us so much that he went back to heaven *as a human!* Think about that for a minute. The *bodily* Jesus is in heaven. There is something of our humanity forever imbedded within God himself. But that was God's plan all along, even before he created you. That is also what Jesus wanted so much--that the effusive, overflowing love of God (Father, Son, and Spirit, a community of love) might be *in us* and we in turn might be *in God* (John 17:20ff). That is also the goal of Paul and Timothy in writing Colossians to us: that we may come "into Jesus" and Jesus might be "in us." This is the only way for us humans to mature to become all that God created us to be. This is

[18]From Timothy Keller, *How to Win the West Again* (New York: Redeemer City to City, 2020), 20-21.

our hope, the hope of glory, the hope of becoming human again.

Encouragement for Daily Living

God wants us to live *hope-filled* lives. He has given us the Scriptures to *encourage* us so that we might have *hope*: "Everything that was written in the past was written to teach us, so that through endurance and encouragement of the Scriptures we might have hope" (Romans 15:4). This book is designed to glean from Colossians encouragement for daily living and reminders of our "hope of glory," which is Christ making his home within each of us. *Not as isolated people*, but rather as people living together with other people in *community.* Jesus has created such a community, a "safe place" of people "*called out*" (Greek, *ekklesia)* from a world of despair to live together in hope.

Passages from Colossians are viewed in "bite-size" doses so that you can read each day and chew on them. There will be a little Greek thrown in so that you can get the flavor of what was originally intended by Paul and Timothy. Each of these daily readings is followed by a prayer so that God will bless your daily meditation. The entire book could be read over 45 days, or it could be savored for a longer period. Discussion questions are included at the end of the book for individual or group study. The Scriptures are amazing if we will spend the time reading, meditating, and listening to what God is telling us.

A few housekeeping notes:

- The text from Colossians at the top of every reading is from the New International Version (NIV), but at times I place in brackets an alternative translation from the English

Standard Version (ESV). Reading various translations of any given text provides rich rewards.

- Whenever the Greek word for Christ appears (*christos*, which in Hebrew is *Messiah*, or anointed one), I most often use the designation, *King*. For the Jews, the Messiah was the long-awaited King of Israel who would become King of the world. For Paul and the early Christians, Jesus was this King, the long awaited (and mysterious) fulfillment of that hope, not just for Israel but for all nations. King Jesus was challenging Caesar and the entire Roman Empire, and the Good News announcement was subversive. But King Jesus was more powerful than Rome or any other power, and King Jesus overcame all the dark "powers" of the culture of the first century, just as he does today. The Kingdom of Jesus marches on, releasing prisoners every day.

- Since Ephesians is so much like Colossians, in some daily readings I will include the parallel passages from Ephesians.

- *We, as humans, become who we are through our habits.* Sprinkled throughout are some "*Walking Habits*," daily practices and habits that will help restore our mental health and humanity and will refocus our vision and hope as humans.[19]

May your reading be blessed, and my prayer is that the Word of God may saturate your mind so that, as Paul prays:

---

[19]A wonderful book that emphasizes coming to know God through what we do ("walking habits") is by James Bryan Smith, *The Good and Beautiful God: Falling in Love with the God Jesus Knows* (Downers Grove, Il: 2009). Many of our "walking habits" will come from Smith's book.

"We haven't stopped praying for you, asking God to give you wise minds and spirits attuned to his will, and so acquire a thorough understanding of the ways in which God works. God rescued us from dead-end alleys and dark dungeons. He's set us up in the kingdom of the Son he loves so much, the Son who got us out of the pit we were in, got rid of the sins we were doomed to keep repeating." (Col. 1:9, 13-14, The Message).

THINGS TO KNOW BEFORE WE BEGIN (A LITTLE BACKGROUND FOR COLOSSIANS)

Before we begin, let me give you a little background, which can go a long way in understanding the letter to the Colossians.

Colossae and the Colossians Christians

The first recipients of this letter were believers in Jesus living in the city of Colossae, a town that sits at the foot of the Cadmus mountains in the heart of present-day Turkey.. Colossae was set in the beautiful Lycus Valley, with the mountains looking down overhead and the Maeander river running through it. At one time, Colossae was a prestigious city known for its wool and textile industry. It was near two other important business centers: Laodicea, ten miles to the east, and Hierapolis, six miles to the north. Most of the people living in Colossae were non-Jewish, a mixture of native people to this region and others who would have immigrated for business and other reasons. The people would have been religious (because everyone was back then), and there seems to have been a mixture of religions in this area: the cultic worship of the Greek gods (now "Romanized" by the Romans), worship of the "great" Artemis of Ephesus (Ephesus was about 100 miles to the east), and the so-called "mystery religions." There were, however, a sizable number of Jews living in this area, which we will see is important in understanding why this letter was written. While at one time Colossae was an important business center, its importance ceased when it was virtually destroyed by an earthquake somewhere between 61 and 64 AD. Given how decimating this earthquake was, Paul and Timothy probably wrote this letter sometime before the earthquake.

Where Were Paul and Timothy Writing From?

Paul and Timothy are writing this letter from a prison cell somewhere. They have never visited the church in Colossae, but they have heard about this young church from a guy named Epaphras, who was from Colossae. Epaphras probably became a Christian through Paul's ministry in nearby Ephesus, sometime between 52 and 55 AD. Paul says Epaphras was the one who first told people in Colossae about Jesus (1:7). Epaphras surely loved the Colossian Christians because Paul says he "wrestles in prayer" for them (4:12). Unfortunately, Epaphras was also in prison with Paul, so Paul had to send his letter by means of a man named Tychicus (who also was the courier of the Ephesian letter), together with a man named Onesimus. Onesimus is interesting because he is a runaway slave, having left the home of a man named Philemon, who also lived in Colossae. Apparently, Onesimus ended up in someplace where Paul was preaching (possibly Ephesus) and had become a Christian. Paul sent a letter to Philemon (along with Onesimus) encouraging Philemon to welcome Onesimus back with open arms as a brother in Christ, and putting pressure on him to release Onesimus from slavery. It is possible that the letter to Philemon and the letter to the Colossians were sent at the same time.

The letter to Colossians is part of what are known as the "Prison Letters" because they were written from a prison cell, the other ones being Philippians, Philemon, and Ephesians. The traditional view is that Paul wrote Colossians from a prison cell in Rome. We know from the book of Acts and tradition that Paul was imprisoned in Rome beginning around 60 or 61 AD (and eventually beheaded outside of Rome around 66 AD). Other possible places where the letter was written include Caesarea, Philippi, and Ephesus. Scot McKnight makes a good case in favor of Ephesus given its proximity to Colossae (which would explain the many times Paul refers to people coming back and forth between Colossae and where he is to visit him) and how closely the letter of Colossians and Ephesians resemble each other.[1] As McKnight concludes, "if Colossians was written from Ephesus, we would need to date the letter in the mid-50s, or perhaps even 57, one date for the riot of Demetrius (Acts 19:23-41)."[2]

Why Were Paul and Timothy Writing?

Paul and Timothy wanted to encourage the young Christians in their faith, particularly to address a certain "philosophy" that was infiltrating the Colossian church. Paul calls this philosophy "hollow" and "deceptive," based on a human understanding (i.e., looking from the world up instead of looking from God's perspective). We get a good picture of what this philosophy

---

[1]Scot McKnight, *The Letter to the Colossians* (Grand Rapids, MI: Eerdmans, 2018), 37-39.
[2]McKnight, 39.

taught in Col. 2:8-23, although Paul and Timothy are subtly attacking it throughout their letter. From what we can piece together, this philosophy taught that true spiritual "knowledge" and "wisdom" were attained through a group identity and philosophy that combined the following elements:

- *Jewish Nationalism.* The philosophy stressed that a person had to adopt Jewish ceremonial obligations, including circumcision, Sabbath keeping, religious holidays, and food laws. All of these Jewish practices were given by God in the Old Testament to confirm God's covenant love to the people of Israel so that they could be a light of hope to all nations. But these Jewish practices were a foreshadowing of the One who would fulfill and complete them, the Jewish Messiah, King Jesus. In Jesus, God is making a covenant of love with all races, nations, and ethnic groups, and thus nationalism of any sort is out of place. What Paul and Timothy were confronting was a claim that Judaism provided "national superiority which Judaism had thought to claim on the basis of God's choice of her. For Paul, the gospel of the crucified and risen Messiah reveals that God has all along had a different end in view. National Israel, with her Law, was simply the preliminary stage in this plan, which always envisaged an eventual world-wide family."[3]
- *A Body-Denying Dualism.* The philosophy also stressed that a heightened spiritual awareness could be achieved through harsh treatment of the body (2:23). The catchphrase of this philosophy was "Do not handle, do not touch, do not taste" (2:21). This is one form of *dualism*, the

[3]N.T. Wright, *Colossians and Philemon* (Downers Grove, Il.: IVP Academic, 1986), 33.

belief that the body and the soul/mind are separate from each other. Dualism was prevalent in Greek philosophy, and especially in the teachings of Plato. The Colossian philosophers were promoting a dualism that the mind must subject the body to extreme harshness to keep it in line and to attain true spiritual awareness. Another form of dualism that Christians encountered in the first century was known as "Gnosticism," a philosophy that claimed a secret and hidden wisdom for the elite, but believed that it didn't matter what you did with your body because your mind and inner self was your true self (which sounds very similar to philosophies of today). Thus, the Gnostics claimed you could engage in all kinds of sexual immorality and still attain Divine knowledge and wisdom with their mind and spirit.[4] Paul and the early Christians countered all this dualism with the understanding that everything God made was good, including the body, and that humans should honor God with their bodies (see 1 Tim. 4:4; 1 Cor. 6:12-20). Our bodies are an important part of who we are, so much so that God himself took on our human body. "Christianity holds that body and soul together form an integrated unity—that the human being is an embodied soul. We respect and honor our bodies as part of the revelation of God's purpose for our lives. The way our bodies function provides rational grounds for our moral decisions."[5]

- *Self-Absorbed Mysticism.* The philosophy also stressed a form of mysticism that sought to attain heightened spiritual awareness, even "worship with angels," and going into de-

[4]Paul confronts this type of Gnostic dualism in the Corinthian church (see, e.g., 1 Cor. 6:12-20), and John confronts this type of Gnostic dualism in 1 John (see, e.g., 1 John 3:4-10).
[5]Nancy R. Pearcy, *Love Thy Body: Answering Hard Questions about Life and Sexuality* (Grand Rapids, MI: Baker, 2018), 21, 23.

tail of "things they have seen" (2:18). The adherents seemed to have been self-absorbed and arrogant because Paul says they are "puffed up with idle notions" (2:18). Paul and Timothy counter that all the fullness of the Divine, God himself, has come to us in Jesus, and that all the wisdom, knowledge, and heightened spiritual experiences we could ever attain are found in Jesus. But when we come to Jesus, we realize that true spirituality is not about attaining self-fulfillment through world-denying "New Age" mysticism. Rather, true spirituality and fullness are found through becoming like Jesus in every way, who selflessly gives himself for others.

- *The Irony of Christianity*. As we will see, the empty and hollow philosophy in Colossae has parallels to the empty and hollow philosophies all around us today. In our readings, we will look at some of these empty philosophies, including *Dualism, Nationalism and Tribalism,* and *Mysticism.* We will see that each of these philosophies *ironically* fails to deliver what they promise. Colossians is full of *irony*: what the philosophers were claiming was ironically found in just the opposite ways of Jesus. And such is the case today, too. Christianity has always been a paradoxical, ironic, "hidden" way to view and live in the world:

  Fullness is found in Christ alone, whereas the philosophy is empty deceit. This fullness does not depend on a heavenly ascent but on a divine descent. Asceticism results in bondage to regulations that thereby makes the participant subject to the flesh. With a world dominated by Platonic categories [dualism], it is ironic to say that those who partook of practices associated with a heavenly ascent were not entering into the reality, but a shadow. Reality is found in Christ alone.[6]

Top Ten Words and Phrases in Colossians

Listed below are Paul's and Timothy's "Top Ten" words and phrases (and associated words), which underscore the rich theological themes in Colossians. These words and phrases provide a good overview of the entire letter. We will explore these in more detail in our daily readings, but for now, be looking for these words and phrases:

1. *Lord and Messiah (King) over all "Powers."* We take for granted the words Paul often uses to describe Jesus—*the Lord Jesus Christ* (1:3). But we need to understand the full impact of what he is saying. Whenever Paul uses the word "Lord" (and he uses it 163 times in his letters and 13 times in Colossians), he is not talking generically about "God." Instead, when Paul uses "Lord" (*Kyrios)*, he is talking about the man Jesus of Nazareth, who was publicly humiliated and murdered on a Roman cross, but most importantly, overcame death itself. Why is this word "Lord" significant? Because it is the same word that is used in the Greek translation of the Old Testament for *Yahweh*, the Creator and God of the universe, who personally revealed himself to the nation of Israel. So, when the early Christians said, "Jesus is Lord!" they were saying "Jesus is God!" When referring to Jesus, Paul and the early Christians used the term "Lord" with another important word, the Hebrew term, "*Messiah*"

---

[6]Ian K. Smith, *Heavenly Perspective: A Study of the Apostle Paul's Response to a Jewish Mystical Movement in Colossae* ((London: T&T Clark, 2006), 144.

(translated into Greek as "Christ"). Messiah means "Anointed One," and was used by the Jews to refer to God's appointed King of Israel. Despite having been conquered by the Babylonians, the Persians, the Greeks and then the Romans, the Jews looked forward to the coming Messiah whom God would place as King of the entire world (see Zech. 14:9). So, when the early Christians said, "Jesus Christ (Messiah)," they were also saying that Jesus was the long-awaited King of Israel and King of the world! Whenever you read the word "Christ," think "King of the world." The claim that "Jesus is Lord!" was also a protest cry. Caesar was not the true Emperor; Jesus was. "For Paul there was one true Lord of the empire; his name was Jesus, and he was the Jewish Messiah."[7]

This isn't an abstract claim, either. Jesus is God and King in the dirty details of your life, and that is where the "powers" come in. Paul and Timothy mention the word "powers" and associated words (like dominion, rulers, and authorities) 8 times in Colossians, and even more so in Ephesians. Who are these "powers," and how has Jesus overcome them? We will delve into this as we explore Colossians, but for now, think about this: *whatever is bringing oppression and darkness in your life is a "power," and Jesus has already triumphed over that power.* Jesus has the greater power to release you and set you free from everything that oppresses you. Jesus has disarmed those powers and has made a "public spectacle" of them, triumphing over them by his cross (2:15). Jesus has taken away all the "power" of those things that make you feel guilty, lonely, depressed, or fearful; he has brought peace to you by bleeding for you (1:20).

---

[7]McKnight, 1.

2. *"In Christ" or "in Him."* A repeated phrase and concept in Colossians (19 times) is the phrase "in Christ," "in him," or "in the Lord" (Paul's favorite phrases, appearing an astounding 164 times in his letters). What does Paul mean when he says we are "in Christ"? Simply put, it means coming into the sphere or realm of protection of Jesus, our God and King. Jesus has rescued us from all oppressive powers, and he implores us to come "into him" for protection and rest. Jesus told his disciples on the night before he was murdered that they must "abide in him" or "remain in Me" (Jn. 15:4,5,9). He was talking specifically about the time *after* his resurrection and ascension to heaven. King Jesus wants us to remain "in him" *now*, during our lives.

3. *"Christ in you."* This is the flip side of being "in Christ." If we remain "in Christ," then Christ will seep into and fill our minds, souls, emotions, and habits. Letting Jesus be "in us" is the second part of what Jesus told us in John 7:56: "Remain in me and *I in you*." When we let Christ penetrate deeper *into us*, we experience "fullness" and we begin to become fully human, all that God originally intended humans to be, patterned after Jesus himself, the "prototype" or blueprint for humanity (1:15).

4. *"Fullness" and "Glory."* Colossians is filled with this idea of "fullness." Paul wants us to have the "full knowledge" of what God has done and is doing in Jesus. All of God's "fullness" (all of who God is) was pleased to be embodied in a human, the man Jesus of Nazareth. Although King Jesus rules from heaven, he is still among us, and in a very real sense he resides bodily here in his church through the members of his body—us! This fullness of God dwells in Jesus so that we, in turn, might have fullness by being in Him and letting Jesus dwell in us.

Tied to the idea of fullness is the word "glory." In the Old Testament, glory referred to the overwhelming, bright presence of God himself. Glory is where God is, where everything is right, true, and beautiful. We humans were meant for that glory, to be glorious creatures. But we have fallen from that glory. The Bible teaches that every human still bears the image of God; our turning away from God (the "Fall") has not taken that away (see, e.g., Gen. 9:6; James 3:9). The fact that God has created every human in his image provides dignity and worth to all humans and should be the bedrock for every society. While every human still bears the image of God, what we have lost is the *glory* God intended for us (Rom. 3:23). The glory is what Jesus restores—he transforms us from one degree of glory to another as we become more like him, the true and perfect image of God (2 Cor. 3:18). *King Jesus is our hope of glory (*1:27).

5. *Jesus is the "Mystery."* Paul uses the word "mystery" (*musterion*) 4 times in Colossians (and 6 times in Ephesians and 20 times in all his letters). *Mystery* is the perfect word to describe what God has done in Jesus and how he has done it. When Paul uses "mystery," he doesn't mean "hard to understand." He means something that was hidden but is now fully disclosed for everyone to know. Jesus is the mystery that God has kept hidden for ages and generations but now disclosed "in its fullness" (1:25; 26). In Jesus, God has unlocked the mystery of humanity; he has revealed exactly how humanity can escape its self-destruction. "Christians believe that not only the mystery of the divine, but also the deepest truths about human life and destiny, have been re-

vealed in Jesus Christ."[8] King Jesus is exactly how each of us, together, may be recreated by God himself to be all that God intended us to be.

6. *Understanding, Wisdom, and Knowledge.* These three words are also constant themes running throughout Colossians (wisdom appearing 6 times, knowledge and "full knowledge" appearing 5 times, and understanding appearing 2 times). The young Colossian church was being plagued by philosophies that were claiming some sort of "secret" or hidden wisdom that only the elite possessed. Paul and Timothy counter that in King Jesus we see the God who created this universe, "in whom are hidden all the treasures of wisdom and understanding" (2:3).

7. *The Body of King Jesus, his Church.* The church is central to Colossians because it is central to God himself. Jesus has so aligned himself with humans that he refers to us as part of his own body. When any part of his body (us) suffers, King Jesus feels that suffering (see Acts 9:4, where Jesus tells Paul that when he persecuted the church, he was persecuting Jesus). The Greek word for church, *ekklessia*, means "called out," and we are the ones called out of this crazy world by God himself into a safe place, an "incubator" where we are loved and where we learn how to love and how to live, how to become human again.

   But the church is more than a social club; it is the place where King Jesus is our model on how to love and live. From him, "the whole body, supported and held together by

[8]Mary Catherine Hilkert, "Cry Beloved Image: Rethinking the Image of God," in *In the Embrace of God: Feminist Approaches to Theological Anthropology*, ed. Ann Elizabeth O'Hara Graff (Maryknoll, NY: Orbis, 1995), 201.

its sinews and ligaments, grows as God causes it to grow" (2:19). Here, in the church, there are no racial, ethnic, gender, or social barriers--King Jesus is all and is in all (3:11). Here, in the church, we experience and learn how to grow in "compassion, kindness, humility, gentleness, and patience" (3:12), forgiving each other just like King Jesus forgave us, teaching each other and encouraging each other with songs from the Spirit and hearts overflowing with gratitude (3:13, 16). The church is not just "part of the journey toward the goal of salvation, but it is intrinsic to the goal itself. There is, there can be, no private salvation, no salvation which does not involve us with one another."[9]

8. *"Faithful" and "fruitful."* The word "faith" appears often in Colossians, but it is better translated as "faithful." We become faithful, trustworthy people because we have experienced the faithful, trustworthy love of God. We become faithful by our *allegiance* to the faithful love of God. In the New Testament, the word "faith" or "belief" does not only mean agreeing with our minds; it also means agreeing with our emotions, our habits, and who we hang out with. Faith means *allegiance*, trust over time. Allegiance means we are daily apprentices or disciples of King Jesus. We commit ourselves to him because he has committed himself forever to us. We commit ourselves to him also because we have come to realize that fullness of life comes about only under and with him.

The fullness that comes by faithfulness leads to "fruit," another important word for Paul in Colossians. The Good News announcement of God's loving faithfulness and power

[9]Leslie Newbigin, *The Gospel in a Pluralist Society* (Grand Rapids: Eerdmans, 1989), 82.

in King Jesus is "bearing fruit" all over the world (and still does!) (1:6). The Gospel has a power all its own; like seed, it will inevitably sprout and grow and produce more fruit if given the right soil (Mark 4). To bear fruit, we need deep roots. The deep roots for us are God's great love ("rooted and grounded in love," as Paul says in Eph. 3:17), and the full knowledge of God he has given us in King Jesus. Daily, over time, our new habits in the apprenticeship of King Jesus will make our lives fruitful and flourishing, producing "fruit that will last" (Jn. 15:16).

9. *"Thankful" and prayerful.* Colossians drips with thanksgiving; our lives should also drip with thanksgiving. Paul constantly repeats the theme of thanksgiving throughout his letter: we mature in our relationship with King Jesus by giving thanks, which can help provide endurance and patience in difficult times (1:12), and we mature in our relationship with King Jesus as we sink down deeply into his love and let his love overflow with thanksgiving (2:7). Being thankful is part of how we let King Jesus bring peace and unity in our community of believers (3:15).

   Giving thanks and prayer are closely connected. Thanksgiving provides fuel for our prayers. Paul sums it up in 4:2 by saying, "Devote yourselves to prayer, being watchful and thankful." Being thankful opens the way for us to see what God is doing in our lives, and maybe especially when we can't see that he is doing anything, when times are difficult. Giving thanks prepares the way for God to show us his salvation (Ps. 50:13, 15).

10. *"Loved"* and *"Grace."* The word love (and its derivatives) occurs 11 times in Colossians, not to mention related words such as "forgiveness" and "reconciliation." The closely re-

lated word "grace" occurs 4 times. In many ways, you could say love and grace are at the heart of Colossians, just as love and grace are in the heart of God himself. A key verse is 3:12, where Paul says that we are chosen by him and "dearly loved." That is ultimately what it means to be human and how to become human again: to be loved. We are indeed loved by the Source of love, the God of the universe. God is a community of love from eternity—Father, Son, and Spirit. He did not need to create us, but because he is love, he created us in love to experience love and to grow in love. He has now rescued us from a hateful, dark world and has transferred us into the authority/power/kingdom of the Son he loves, in whom we have forgiveness and through whom we experience this redeeming love.

By coming under the protection of God's love (and in his community of loved ones), we grow in love and learn how to love others better. The world sees and notices how much we love each other, and they want that, too. We take these ways of love we have learned in the incubator of the church and spread the aroma of grace everywhere we go, so that our conversations with outsiders are always "full of grace" (4:6).

Now that we have looked at the background to Colossians and some of its key themes, let's begin our journey, walking daily with King Jesus through Colossians.

DAILY WALKS

WHO IS WRITING THIS LETTER?

Paul, an apostle of Christ Jesus by the will of God, and Timothy our brother,

2 To God's holy people [saints] in Colossae, the faithful brothers and sisters in Christ:

Grace and peace to you from God our Father. (1:1,2)

Letter writers in the first century would begin by stating *who they were* and *who they were writing to.* This letter is written by two people, early followers of Jesus, who shared a close bond created by Jesus. The letter is written to a young church in a small town located in present day Turkey, about 1,000 miles from where Christianity first began in Jerusalem. The message of Jesus was spreading like wildfire throughout the Middle East and to the ends of the world.

Who Wrote This Letter?

The first named writer is Paul, the same man who used to be called Saul, raised in the strictest of Jewish Orthodox sects (the Pharisees), zealous for everything "God." When the disciples of Jesus (that blasphemous teacher who claimed to be divine) began persuading others to follow Jesus by proclaiming that he had been miraculously raised from the dead, Paul would have none of it! He went from town to town, locking Christians up in jail, breathing "murderous threats" (Acts 9:1). But on one of those trips, he was stopped in his tracks by none other than the Risen Jesus! Jesus of Nazareth was indeed alive, but no longer bound by time or space. God was still working his good will through humans (just like he had done from the time of Noah and Abraham), but now God was working out his mysterious, ancient plan of transforming humans and cultures the world over.

After this encounter with Jesus, Paul had to get away by himself for a while, and he went into Arabia for about three years (Gal. 1:17, 18). It was probably during this time that God began putting all the pieces together for Paul. Paul began to understand the ancient "will of God" revealed in King Jesus:

- Jesus of Nazareth is none other than God assuming flesh and bones.
- Jesus was not "Plan B" in God's will, but Jesus was always "Plan A" from before time began.
- Jesus has revealed who "God" is, and God is a community of self-giving love: Father, Son, and Spirit, who created us in love for love.
- Jesus (the Son of God) created everything and everyone, so humans (created by Jesus) find their true selves through knowing God revealed in Jesus.
- Jesus is not only the "prototype" of what God intended for humans, but God also "recreates" humans through the Spirit of Jesus and his church to become all God intended us to be.

- This "recreation" of humanity is for everyone the world over, as God's love transcends all barriers of race and culture, creating a multi-ethnic community.
- This is all "good news," and God's "will" is for humans to flourish (or as Paul would say, "bear fruit" and come to "fullness" in Jesus).

Paul didn't make all this up; as he told the Galatian Christians, he received all this by revelation from King Jesus (Gal. 1:12). Paul underscores this at the beginning of his letter to the Colossians by describing himself as an "apostle of King Jesus *by the will of God*." Paul wants these Christians in Colossae to be filled with the same "knowledge of the will of God" (1:9). This knowledge is not just information about King Jesus; it is the experiential knowledge of the personal presence of Jesus within a community which results in changed, fruitful and flourishing lives. Paul was never the same after he met Jesus, and he knows that when you open yourself up to the Spirit of the Living King Jesus, nothing will be the same for you either.

Let's not forget the other writer, Timothy. More than likely, Timothy was actively involved in writing this letter with Paul (just as he was with the other letters that also bear his name—Philippians, 1 and 2 Thessalonians, 2 Corinthians, and Philemon). Paul and the early Christians believed in *shared power* and *collaborative ministry*. They learned this from King Jesus himself, who sent out his followers "two by two" and who repeatedly told them that the greatest among them was the one who serves. Timothy was a perfect "co-minister" of this new Gospel message because he was from a mixed-race family: his mother was Jewish, and his father was a Gentile (possibly a Roman). But for Paul the Jew, Timothy was his "brother."

Already we are beginning to see from this letter that the "will of God" is that we be in community with others, a *family* of all different races and cultures. God our Father beautifully blends our different cultures and ethnic backgrounds, weaving them into a tapestry through self-giving love, all learned from the greatest Giver, King Jesus. Although Paul and Timothy wrote this letter together, I will sometimes only reference Paul for simplicity's sake. But don't forget Timothy!

†

God, whose heart is that of a tender Father, and King Jesus, the perfect expression of the Father's love, thank you today for your Word that can open our eyes and enlighten our hearts and minds so that we may know you better. Today, I thank you for the people in my life. Thank you that you didn't create us to live alone but to be connected with others. Bring new friendships in my life and deepen old ones. Help me to relish and appreciate conversations and time together with others. Help me see better the people in my life that can come along beside and help me, and help me to notice and help those that I can come along beside and encourage. In the name of King Jesus, amen.

WHO ARE THEY WRITING TO?

Paul, an apostle of Christ Jesus by the will of God, and Timothy our brother,

2 To God's holy people [saints] in Colossae, the faithful brothers and sisters in Christ:

Grace and peace to you from God our Father. (1:1,2)

Paul and Timothy were writing to a young Christian church in a predominantly pagan, Gentile territory, although there were many Jews who lived in or near Colossae. They have never visited this young church, but their friend Epaphras has told them about the Christians in Colossae. In fact, word is getting out about the explosion of Christianity throughout this region. Paul and Timothy describe who they are writing to with words that speak to us today:

- *"Holy people" or "saints."* The word "holy" didn't originally mean "pure" or "good." It meant "separated, different, special." It described things used in temple worship, things that were not for everyday use but for sacred, special purposes. What made them holy was what they were devoted to—the worship of God. By being devoted to God, something of common use (like a dish or cup) was made holy. The same idea applies to us: we are not holy in ourselves, but we immediately become holy when God chooses us by his grace and cleanses us by his love. But as we devote ourselves to God, we become holy, set apart for special purposes (actually, purposes God always intended for us). As the writer of Hebrews says, God has already made holy those who are *in the process of becoming holy* (Heb. 10:14). When you think about it, holiness is what each of us want deep down. As David Brooks writes, "We don't live for happiness, we live for holiness. Day to day we seek pleasure, but deep down, human beings are endowed with moral imagination. All human beings seek to lead lives not just for pleasure, but of purpose, righteousness, and virtue. Life is essentially a moral drama, not a hedonistic one."[1] Walter Brueggemann writes, "The Bible asserts that this coming of God's holiness is the deepest yearning and the most powerful craving we have. We are made for God's holiness, and it is exactly God's holiness that makes us human. It is the glory of God and the wonder of God that makes our life joyously whole. That is the truth about us."[2]

- *"Faithful."* The Colossians were not just "full of faith," they were "faithful." Faithful means *allegiance* or trust over time. They had trusted over time in the faithfulness of God, which in turn made them faithful, loyal people. This is really what being a "believer" means. Faith in Jesus is not just mental assent to certain propositions; it is being gripped by the grace of God who never gives up on us, and holding on for dear life. By constantly holding on to Jesus, we start taking on his same character of faithfulness. As

---

[1]David Brooks, *The Road to Character* (New York: Random House, 2015), 262.
[2]Walter Brueggemann, *A Gospel of Hope* (Louisville: Westminster John Knox Press, 2018), 79.

Paul put it in Philippians 3:12, "I'm not perfect, but I press on to take hold of that for which King Jesus took hold of me." By being in community with other faithful people, we see what faith looks like—we become faithful to others and others are faithful to us. A great example is Epaphras: the Colossians saw this character trait of faithfulness from him, who first told them about Jesus (1:7). Who in your life has been faithful to you? Who in your life needs you to be faithful to them?

- *"Brothers and sisters."* Believers in Jesus are not just a group of people meeting in a certain place. We are *family*, a family created by Father God. In ancient times, the strongest ties were family ties between brothers and sisters. Jesus took that bond to an even deeper level. The bonds of love and kinship created in Jesus run even deeper than biological love. This Christian family in Colossae was comprised of different races (Gentiles and Jews), genders (Nympha was a house church leader), and socio-economic levels (slaves and free). "One suspects Paul's multi-ethnic vision for the church is taking root already in Colossae, for in [chapter 4] we have a Jew writing to a Gentile-dominated church where there is a slave (4:9) and a doctor (4:14), all meeting in the home of a woman householder (4:15)."[3]

- *"In Colossae" and "in Christ."* Believers in Jesus are both in a certain place but always "in Christ." The phrases "in Christ," "in Him," and "in the Lord" are among Paul's favorites, using them 164 times in his letters and 19 times in Colossians. Paul uses interchangeably the phrases "in Christ" and "Christ in you," echoing what Jesus told his disciples: "Remain in me, as I remain in you" (John 15:4).

---

[3]McKnight, 382.

> To be "in Christ" is to come into the "sphere" of Jesus, his sphere of acceptance, forgiveness, grace, wisdom, maturity, protection, and confidence. Jesus promised that if we remain "in him," then we will live fruitful, flourishing lives ("fruit that will last") (John 15:1-17). Being and remaining "in Christ" opens the door for Christ to be "in you," for Jesus to "dwell in your hearts through faith," for God's love to be "poured into your hearts," for God's Spirit to make connection with your spirit so that you cry out in love, "Abba, Father," so that the joy of Jesus may be in you and your joy may be complete! (see Eph. 3:17, Rom. 5:5, Gal. 4:6, John 15:11). This all happens in a particular *place.* While the church is a worldwide phenomenon, we each live in a particular city or town, and King Jesus calls each of us to a particular group of believers in that particular city or town. "To be described as 'in Christ' and 'in Colossae' is to be located with precision in the purposes of God, as a member both of his true people and of that particular earthly community where one is called to service and witness."[4]

Paul finishes his opening with a greeting, but the greeting actually comes from God himself. To paraphrase:

> *God your Father says hello with his grace, which brings peace.*

Jews would greet each other by saying *Shalom*, which means peace. What they meant by Shalom was not just an absence of conflict, but "well-being," "flourishing and thriving." Such well-being comes only from Creator God. Paul combines this Jewish greeting with the beautiful Christian word, *Grace*

[4]Wright, *Colossians*, 50-51.

(*karis*). Creator God is the one who brings both well-being and grace; he brings his well-being through grace. God is the initiator of peace, the reconciler of all of our conflicts (internal and external), making peace by the blood of his cross (1:20). Grace and peace are what we as humans long for, and grace and peace are what our *Abba* Father brings to us through Jesus, the King of Peace and the Giver of Grace.

†

Father God and our King Jesus, thank you so much for being faithful to me, even when I didn't and don't deserve your faithfulness. You are like a Rock, always there, always pursuing my heart, always wanting what is best for me. Thank you especially for teaching me, by your faithful love, how to be a faithful person. Right now, I thank you for the people in my life who have made a difference by being faithful to me. I also think about people to whom I need to be faithful, and I bring them before you now. Fill me with your supernatural, energizing love and give me the same faithful commitment to them that you, Jesus, have for me. Praise be to your character—to who you are!

THREE KEYS TO BECOMING HUMAN AGAIN

We always thank God, the Father of our Lord Jesus Christ, when we pray for you, 4 because we have heard of your faith in Christ Jesus and of the love you have for all God's people— 5 the faith and love that spring from the hope stored up for you in heaven and about which you have already heard in the true message of the gospel 6 that has come to you [the word of the truth, the gospel that has come to you]. (1:3-6)

As he often does, Paul begins this letter by giving thanks. This opening thanksgiving is strikingly similar to how he opens his letter to Philemon. Being thankful is a key theme throughout the Colossian letter (see 1:12; 2:6; 3:15, 16,17; 4:2). Paul shows by example and by exhortation that our lives will be different and more joyful if we just remember to give thanks every day. "The root of joy is gratefulness…It is not joy that makes us grateful; it is gratitude that makes us joyful."[1] Prayer becomes the empowering encounter with God when it is filled with thanksgiving. "What God has done is always the 'perch'

---

[1]David Steindl-Rast, *Gratefulness: The Heart of Prayer* (New York: Paulist Press/Ramsey, 1984), 204.

(so to speak) from which Christian prayer takes its flight and to which it returns."[2]

Although Paul and Timothy have never been to Colossae or nearby Laodicea, news about this young church has spread. The news about King Jesus was being listened to and taken seriously in Colossae and throughout the Roman Empire, and was dynamically changing people. Word had gotten out that people were free from oppression and were living thriving, confident, sacrificial lives. The hallmarks of this change were the three traits that came to be the "code words" of Christianity, words that were so strange to the ears of Greeks and Romans in the first century but words our secular culture now takes for granted: *faith, love, and hope* (Paul uses this trio often). These three are not so much what we do as *who we are*, *who we become* over time as Jesus transforms us. To become human is to have faith and become faithful; to be loved and learn how to love; and to possess something that gives us hope and become hopeful people. Faith, hope, and love bring fullness to our lives, and from these three traits flow what we do, fruit that lasts over the long haul. Let's look at each:

Becoming Human means possessing in increasing measure:

1. *Faith in King Jesus.* Christian faith is not simply an intellectual belief in a set of doctrines. It is a growing allegiance to a very personal God who invades every part of your life—your mind, your emotions, your body, your will, your social connections, your past, present, and future. We don't have faith "about Jesus," we have faith "in Jesus." We have faith in Jesus not only because God has, at a particular point in time and history, come to us in human form, experiencing

[2]C.F.D. Moule, *The Phenomenon of the New Testament* (London: SCM Press, 1967), 48.

everything we go through (even death). We have faith in Jesus because he rose from the dead and is present, as a Spiritual Presence, in our lives *now*. When life was dark, the Personal Presence of God broke through, more real than the air we breathe. When we were dead in our souls, "God made us alive with Christ," he "rescued us from the dominion of darkness" and brought us into a free and open space, "the kingdom of the Son he loves" (2:13, 1:13). From our darkness, God "raised us up with Christ" and *right now, right this minute*, King Jesus has seated us right next to him, far above all the dark powers of this world (Eph. 2:6). Allegiance to the Personal Presence of the Spirit of God in Jesus frees us from fear, from those powers that corrupt and oppress us. Allegiance to the love of Jesus trains us to live self-controlled, fruitful lives in this present age while we wait for the blessed hope, the full revelation of all that God has done and is doing in Jesus (Titus 2:12).

2. *Love for All Kinds of People*. What we humans most need is to be loved and learn how to love others better. So, what's the problem—why is that so hard? There are many reasons, but mostly because we are selfish, because we are afraid (what if they don't love me back?), and because we have been hurt in the past and our wounds make it hard to love. What we need is a love "big enough" to heal us, fill us, and change us. God himself is that "Big Love" that fills us with his Personal Presence: "God has poured his love into our hearts through his Spirit" (Rom. 5:5). The Colossians had felt this love of God pouring into their hearts: "Epaphras told us of your love in the Spirit" (Col. 1:8). There is such a "Big Love," and Jesus is the full expression of the sacrificial, suffering, faithful love of God. Jesus is the ultimate expression of the faithful, covenant love of God shown

throughout the Old Testament. As Scot McKnight says, God's covenant love is "a commitment of presence, advocacy, and protection, and his commitment entails both summoning his people into, and providing for, their transformation into Christlikeness."[3]

Love is not an abstract concept; we understand love in human faces, through hugs, listening, caring. Being in a *community*, which God calls *the body of Christ*, is very much a part of our "salvation," our rescue, what we need and how we become more human. But this community is different; we are all brothers and sisters with our own particular hang-ups and hurts, all rescued solely because of God's great love. And Jesus has taught us that the "greatest" among us is the least, the one who serves, like Jesus does us. Again, Jesus "opens the space" for us to be free to love, free from our past, and free from the people who have hurt us. In this "open space," his kingdom, there is redemption, the forgiveness of sins, and reconciliation (1:14, 22). Jesus's community is comprised of people from all ethnic and cultural backgrounds, all of us different. Being part of a diverse community forces us to learn to love like Jesus: "The Gentile mission forced Jews to love Gentiles, males to love females, slaves to love the free, and Scythians were to love barbarians (Col. 3:11)."[4]

3. *Hope Breaking In.* In a sense, without the hope that we have in the loving, risen Jesus, our faith would be futile (1 Cor. 15:14). But our faith is not futile because the crucified Jesus really did rise from the dead. Because of Jesus, history is going somewhere. We have hope because we have come to

---

[3]McKnight, 93.
[4]Id.

understand that the covenant faithfulness of God is the center of all reality. But the hope that we have as believers is not some far off dream, a wish that after we die, we will "go to heaven." When we die, we will certainly be with Jesus, and so hope is future oriented. But what makes this hope real and alive is that the future is breaking into and transforming the present. It's not that God "gets us into heaven," but that God gets heaven into us. Paul says we have faith in King Jesus, and we love sacrificially because of the "hope being stored for you in the heavens" (1:5). But this same future hope is also "Christ in you" now, the hope of glory (1:27). As Marianne Thompson says:

> The future—God's action for our salvation—has reached into the present, and it is this in-breaking of the revelation of God's glory, of the promises 'kept for you in heaven,' that gives hope in the present, hope that the situation of the world will be transformed, and that God has not abandoned the world to its own devices. For Paul, hope does not simply have to do with the end. It also has to do with the beginning of life in Christ, for such life always lives in and with the hope that the world does not determine its own course and that the death-dealing ways of the world are not the final word written over it.[5]

†

I thank you again, my God and Father and the Father of King Jesus, for how faithful you have been to me. You have become real to me because you have never given

[5]Marianne Meye Thompson, *Colossians & Philemon* (Grand Rapids, MI: Eerdmans, 2005), 22.

up on me. Your faithful love makes me unafraid and at peace. Your faithful love also teaches me how to love. Remind me that you created me to be in community with others, and that I am most fully alive when I am with others and helping others. Give me your courage to do the next thing I need to do to get more connected with people. Thank you for the hope of the quality, forever kind of life breaking into my heart and life now in the face of your Son, my King Jesus. Praise your name, Lord Jesus! Amen.

TRUTH AND GRACE SPROUT A FLOURISHING LIFE

...the faith and love that spring from the hope stored up for you in heaven and about which you have already heard in the true message of the gospel 6 that has come to you [the word of truth, the gospel that has come to you]. In the same way, the gospel is bearing fruit and growing throughout the whole world—just as it has been doing among you since the day you heard it and truly understood God's grace [understood the grace of God in truth]. (1:5, 6)

The message of Jesus came to you so that you could flourish and thrive. Jesus said, "I have come that they may have life (*zoe*, or quality life), and have it to the full!" (John 10:10). What are humans for? To *flourish*, or as Jesus and Paul would say to "bear fruit," to live fruitful lives. What Jesus is after is not simply "happiness" which depends on circumstances, but deep-down *joy* that will not change when things are difficult. God wants to implant into your heart a joy that can face and even transform difficult times. Jesus is not wanting to help you improve your resume or make your life run more smoothly or more efficient. What he wants is to produce fruit in your life that has a lasting impact and a deep down joy that nothing can take away (see John 15:4-17).

In this passage, Paul tells us that the seeds that will produce a fruitful, flourishing life are *truth* and *grace*, which in Jesus cannot be separated. There is no truth without grace, and there is no grace without Jesus telling the truth about our world and our lives. Two times in these 2 verses, Paul mentions truth and grace: the Gospel (the good news announcement about Jesus) is the word of truth; and when people understand and receive the grace of God in truth, a dynamic explosion begins that will lead to flourishing in their lives and relationships.

The Greek word for Gospel, *euongellion*, was used by the Romans to announce a Roman military victory. When Rome conquered a territory, the Good News (*euongellion*) was announced. The Christians adopted this word to announce the Good News that Jesus had overcome the greatest enemy, death! But Jesus' victory was a victory that "worked backwards."[1] Not only did Jesus overcome death, but he overcame all the dark powers of oppression in this world that enslave us to fear, addiction, guilt, loneliness—all the "death dealing ways" of this world. Paul says understanding what Jesus has done and is able to do in turning people's lives around is spreading like a vibrant, flourishing vine, sending shoots throughout the world and producing fruit inside people's hearts.

How does the Good News of God's grace and truth in Jesus produce fruitful or flourishing lives? How can your life and your relationships become more flourishing? To answer these questions, consider this: *how does fruit grow?* Fruit grows when a seed is deeply implanted in the soil and nourished, watered, and given sunlight. Fruit doesn't grow overnight; it takes time and attention. But patient nourishing, watering, and exposure to the sun will surely, in time, produce fruit. Jesus promises the same in your life and relationships. Constantly receiving

---

[1]From C.S. Lewis, *The Great Divorce* (New York: HarperOne, 1946), 69.

the grace and truth that are only found in Jesus will, in time, produce joy and fruit in your life, joy that nothing can take away and fruit that will last.

How to be Nourished by Truth and Grace

Humans were created to be nourished by both truth and grace. In his book, *The God-Shaped Brain: How Changing Your View of God Transforms Your Life*, Dr. Timothy Jennings describes how our brains are divided into left and right hemispheres. The left side controls our reasoning side, while the right side controls our relational and creative side. Although they have different functions, the hemispheres of our brain are designed to work together. When our brains are imbalanced (one side dominating the other), our lives can become imbalanced. Dr. Jennings notes that *meditating*, that is, daily thinking deeply about both the truth and love of God, can nourish and feed our brain, creating a healthy mind and attitude.

The Bible tells us that the Holy Spirit is both truth and love. Truth is comprehended via the left hemisphere of the brain, whereas our sense of unity, oneness and relational connectedness is experienced in the right side of our brains. God calls us to meditate on his law of love, which is an expression of his character of love. This is no empty, mindless, thoughtless meditation, but a contemplative, deeply reflective meditation on the beauty of our infinite God and his methods of love. Such meditation requires the balanced engagement of both right and left hemispheres. Such balance not only results in greater health and peace but also growth in Christlikeness.[2]

---

[2]Timothy R. Jennings, M.D., *The God-Shaped Brain: How Changing Your View of God Transforms Your Life* (Downers Grove, Il: IVP Press, 2013), 225-226.

Dr. Jennings prescribes the following practices to heal our brains and maintain mental health, as well as provide the seeds to lead to flourishing, fruitful lives:[3]

- Worshipping a God of love and rejecting God-concepts that induce fear.
- Regular meditation on some aspect of God's character of love, at least fifteen minutes per day.
- Being truthful and eliminating falsehood of any kind from the mind.
- Live to give. Actively seek to help others; get involved in some ministry or volunteer activity.
- Establish relationships with people of loving and mature character, and terminate destructive and exploitive relationships.
- Trust God with your life and your life's outcomes.
- Live in harmony with the physical design protocols for life, such as regular sleep, drink plenty of water, exercise mind and body regularly, avoid toxins, and eat a balanced diet.
- When mistakes are made, resolve guilt as soon as possible, forgive those who mistreat you, and don't hold anger or grudges.
- Resolve fear, as unremedied fear truly destroys.

†

Father God, King Jesus, Spirit of Love and Truth, thank you that you are real, alive, and active. Thank you for

[3]These prescribed "medications" are taken verbatim from Jennings, 57-58.

making yourself known through grace and truth. I need both in my life. I am refreshed as I meditate on your selflessness, patience, faithfulness, kindness, goodness, gentleness, and also your truth-telling love for me. By the courage your love gives, help me to give up the lies and falsehoods in my life and run to the Truth, the Truth that sets me free. I am thrilled by your love and the freedom of your Truth!

WALKING HABIT: BEGIN TO PRAY—MEDITATE ON THE GOODNESS OF GOD

The first, and maybe most important, "Walking Habit" is *prayer*. Prayer will be the first, middle, and last Walking Habit because of how important the practice of prayer is. Prayer is conversation and encounter with God.[4] Prayer is connecting our hearts, souls, mind, emotions, relationships—everything we are and do—with the Reality that is God. "Prayer is also the main way we experience deep change—the reordering of our loves. Prayer is simply the key to everything we need to do and be in life."[5] Prayer is not always easy; prayer is a "practice" that we grow into. Meditation on the goodness of God through reading God's Word prepares us to pray; it reminds us of just Who we are talking to. As you begin to grow in the practice of prayer, read passages from the Word that prepare your heart and mind. The Psalms are great, as well as passages that tell us about the heart of God, like Exodus 34:4-7; Psalms 103; Philippians 2:6-11; and Romans 8:28-39. "Meditation is taking the truth down into our hearts until it catches fire there and be-

---

[4]Timothy Keller, *Prayer: Experiencing Awe and Intimacy with God* (New York: Penguin, 2014), 5.
[5]Keller, *Prayer*, 18.

gins to melt and shape our reactions to God, ourselves, and the world."[6]

---

[6]Keller, *Prayer,* 151.

WHAT IS TRUTH?

...about which you have already heard in the true message of the gospel 6 that has come to you [the word of truth, the gospel that has come to you]. In the same way, the gospel is bearing fruit and growing throughout the whole world—just as it has been doing among you since the day you heard it and truly understood God's grace [understood the grace of God in truth]. (1:5-6)

And you were included in Christ when you heard the message of truth, the gospel of your salvation. ...when you heard about Christ and were taught in him in accordance with the truth that is in Jesus. (Eph. 1:13; 4:21)

Is there such a thing as "truth" that applies to all human conduct? Not in the world we live in today. Here are some observations about our current cultural climate:

- *No Absolutes.* Our postmodern world is deeply suspicious of absolutes. Sometimes this suspicion is justified; history usually is written by the victors, and our past (and the traditions we inherit) should be carefully and rationally scrutinized. But unfortunately, today there is little rational discussion when it comes to the question of truth. In our world today, what is true for you might not be "true" for me.

- *Truth is What We Feel.* This current attitude about truth is what philosopher Alasdair MacIntyre called "emotivism," that is, moral judgments are nothing more than emotional expressions of preference.[1]
- *The Abyss of Uncertainty.* This attitude that "truth is a preference" has led to a feeling of instability--there is nothing "solid" about reality. Sociologists have noted this about our postmodern world and have called it by various names, such as "the vertigo of reality," the "abyss of uncertainty," and "liquid modernity."[2] Life and values are like a shopping mall with too many and too uncertain choices. Some sociologists believe this has led to the pervading sense of meaninglessness that is plaguing our Western culture and is contributing to higher suicide rates. Emile Durkheim, in his book *Suicide,* concluded that the primary cause of suicide is not suffering but disequilibrium: "When societal values rapidly change…people lose the ability to clearly evaluate their lives."[3]
- *Power Becomes All-Important.* Another result of "truth is preference" is the current angry divisiveness in society and politics. If truth is just a preference, then *power* becomes all important. "Morality turns out to be the assertion of

---

[1]Alistair MacIntyre, *After Virtue: A Study in Moral Theory*, 2nd ed. (Notre Dame, IN: University of Notre Dame Press, 1984).
[2]See David Lyon, *Postmodernity* (Minneapolis: University of Minnesota Press, 1994), 61.
[3]Noble, 91, citing Emile Durkheim, *Suicide: A Study in Sociology,* ed. George Simpson, trans. John A. Spaulding and George Simpson (New York: Free Press, 1979), 252.

> someone's will upon someone else—an exercise of power, not truth."[4]

Although "truth" (when referring to morality and values) is uncertain in our current culture, there still is such a thing as what is "true" and what is a "lie." We don't like to be lied to, and if people don't tell the truth, then we can't trust them. The lack of truth brings fearfulness and divisiveness. A huge problem in our society today is that people don't tell the *truth*. When you listen to cable news, you don't get the whole truth, you get a slanted version of the truth. Why? Power and money. Our world is much like the world of the ancient prophets: "Truth has fallen in the streets" (Isa. 59:14).

Some Truths About "My Truth"

Truth (as opposed to falsehood) is critical in every discipline (whether math, science, history, business). In every area of our lives, rational, logical inquiry is important. The same should also apply to our search for "truth" when it comes to morality and values. And so, using our logical reasoning ability, let me mention some "truths" about the prevailing cultural attitude that says "truth is my truth."

- Whether people realize it or not, when they say, "there are no absolutes," they are making an "absolute" claim. Saying "what is true for you is not true for other people" is a logical absurdity because when you say this, you are making a truth claim. How do you know if there is no "objective truth"?

---

[4]Noble, 29.

- We often fail to realize how much our thinking about anything has been influenced by our past. All of us are conditioned by history, our communities, our ethnic backgrounds, and our cultural heritage. This is especially so when those who reject Judeo-Christian values fail to realize where many of their "values" came from. As Rebecca McLauglin writes, "To our 21st century, Western ears, love across racial and cultural differences, the equality of men and women, and the idea that the poor, oppressed, and marginalized can make moral claims on the strong, rich, and powerful sound like basic moral common sense. But they are not. These truths have come from Christianity. Rip that foundation out, and you won't uncover a better basis for human equality and rights. You'll uncover an abyss that cannot tell you what a human being is."[5]

Can We Find Truth?

In all this uncertainty, is there any place we can begin to think about "truth?" *Yes!*

We postmoderns are not the first to have considered the question of "What is truth?" Greek and Roman philosophers spent centuries considering the question, and they realized that in order to answer the question, you need the right starting point. As philosopher Alistair MacIntyre points out, these ancients began with the most important question that we postmoderns have thrown out the window: *What is the "telos" (Greek for "goal") or "best ends" for us as humans?*[6]

---

[5]Rebecca McLaughlin, *The Secular Creed: Engaging Five Contemporary Claims* (Austin: The Gospel Coalition, 2021), 2.
[6]MacIntyre, *After Virtue*, 220.

When it comes to morality and values, the question of "truth" is a "*human*" question: What are the things that are best for us as humans, that lead to human flourishing? To begin to understand if there is any objective truth, we need to ask these questions:

- What are human beings, and how do our minds, bodies, and emotions make up our "humanity"? *Are there morals and values that best fit us as humans?*
- What brings about the *flourishing* of humans, both individually and for society, both now and for future generations? *Are there morals and values that best make for the flourishing of human life?*
- Where is this story of humanity going? *Are there morals and values that help us as humans attain the highest goals to which we as humans aspire?*

These are the big questions to ask in understanding "What is Truth?" We find the answers to these questions, though, by realizing that Truth is not a "What," but a "Who?" We will explore that question tomorrow.

†

Creator God, I praise you that I don't have to live in the "abyss of uncertainty" about life. Creator God, you made the world, bringing order out of chaos. You are Truth, and I can rest peacefully on your rock-solid Truth. I can rest peacefully because all that you created reflects that you are not just Creator God, you are Father God, a God of personal love and commitment. You are God the Son, the perfect expression of your faithful, sacrificial love for me and all of your creation. You are Spirit God, the Spirit of Truth and Grace, who recreates in my heart all that brings good, truthful things in my life. Praise you, Elohim (Creator God) and Yahweh (Personal God), my Father, my Lord Jesus, the Spirit of Grace and Truth.

WHO IS TRUTH? (THE TRUE QUESTION OF TRUTH)

...about which you have already heard in the true message of the gospel 6 that has come to you [the word of truth, the gospel that has come to you]. In the same way, the gospel is bearing fruit and growing throughout the whole world—just as it has been doing among you since the day you heard it and truly understood God's grace [understood the grace of God in truth]. (1:5, 6)

Jesus is the one we proclaim...the mystery of God, that is King Jesus, in whom are hidden all the treasures of wisdom and knowledge. (Col. 1:28; 2:3)

Pilate, the Roman proconsul in Jerusalem in the 1st century, asked one of the most controversial, and most important, questions we humans ask: *"What is truth?"* (John 18:38).

That is the way we usually ask the question. But those who come to know the truth realize that "what is truth" is not the right question. "What" is not the *true way* to know the truth about us. But Pilate was a prophet (and didn't know it) because a few minutes later, he answered his own question about what truth is. But before we hear his answer, think for a minute about some of the answers to the question, "What is truth?"

that we can all agree upon, and think about where these answers came from.

Most people would agree that there is "truth" in such values as love, equality, the dignity and worth of all humans, freedom, and concern for the marginalized. But where did all these values originate? They didn't come out of thin air. Out of all the philosophies and religions in the world, these values have their unique origins in the God of the Old Testament. This God was unlike all other gods, a God who is concerned about every human being, and particularly the outcast and marginalized. These very "human," loving and personal values came from a "comprehensive vision of truth" that understands reality as very *personal.*

Truth is Personal

For the ancient Hebrews, "truth" was not some abstract thought; truth is *personal.* The Hebrew word for "truth" (*emet*) means not just "true" but "truthful, *reliable, trustworthy.*" Truth is grasped and understood in a relationship with the God of love, who gives us "truth" for our own good (Deut.10:12,13). The God revealed in the Old Testament is both full of faithful love (*hesed*) and truth (*emet*). He speaks to us personally, and speaks the truth to us for our own good and flourishing. Grace and truth cannot be separated because both come from a personal God who loves us, and God will not lie to us about reality.

In Hebrew, the word for truth, *emet,* consists of three letters, containing the first, middle, and last letters of the Hebrew alphabet. This symbolizes that God's "truth" encompasses all reality. But if you take away the first letter, *aleph* (which represents God), you spell the Hebrew word for death, meaning that without God there is no truth, only death and meaninglessness. The writer of Ecclesiastes begins his book with the word, "Meaningless!" (*hebel*, meaning vapor or pointless). His point is that without God, life is meaningless. But the beauty of the God of the Hebrews was that life made sense when we are in relationship with him. Reality finds its stability in a Creator who created this beautiful, amazing universe in a way that scientists now say is exquisitely "fine-tuned" for humans to exist: "The heavens declare the glory of God" (Ps. 19:1). This amazing, fine-tuned universe came about by the *personal* Creator speaking, communicating; the "Word of God" created this amazing universe out of chaos.

The Word of God also brings order out of our chaotic lives by speaking the Truth into our hearts: "The Word [Torah] of Yahweh is perfect, reviving the soul" (Ps. 19:7). The truly happy person is the one that listens to this Word from God about how to live well; she is like a tree planted by streams of water which flourishes and thrives (Ps. 1).

How Can we Know God is Trustworthy and Reliable?

The personal Creator revealed in the Old Testament answers the question, "Why can we believe what the Bible says is best for humans?" The answer: *because the Creator God who speaks to us is trustworthy and reliable.*

Which leads to a deeper question: *But how can we know God is trustworthy and reliable?*

The full answer to that is found in this suffering servant Pilate presented to the world.

Pilate had been interrogating Jesus of Nazareth, a radical teacher who had claimed to reveal, in his humanness, all of who God is—the very heart and words of God himself. Jesus claimed that God was a Father, and that he revealed this Father God exactly (Jn. 12:49). To the Jews, this was sheer blasphemy. God is the Almighty, the Unapproachable, and no human should dare make such claims! They wanted Jesus put to death. Pilate reluctantly agreed. He had Jesus flogged with whips (excruciating torture which often brought death), and then the soldiers beat Jesus on the face with their fists. Then, in mockery, they jammed a crown of thorns on his head and put a royal, purple robe on him.

Pilate presents this bloody, beaten, humiliated Jesus to the world, and in answering his own question of "what is truth?" proclaims: *"Behold, the human!* (Greek, *anthropos*)." Unknowingly, Pilate declares that this suffering *human,* who claims to be the full revelation of God, is the Truth for us humans.

How can we know God is trustworthy and reliable?

By looking to Jesus, the full expression of God's extravagant love for humans. The real question for us humans is not "What is Truth?" but "*Who is Truth?*"

Who is Truth?

We can begin to understand the question of truth for our lives when we realize that before "Truth" is some set of concepts, doctrines, or beliefs, it is first of all *personal and relational. Truth is always personal because God is always personal and relational, full of compassionate love. God knows what is best for us as the humans he created, and he is willing to go to whatever lengths to bring us into relationship with him.*

The personal God of faithful love (*hesed*) and truthfulness (*emet*) was true to himself when he came to fully dwell with us as humans. No one has ever seen God, but God has made himself known (Jn. 1:18). The Word that created the universe, that speaks into our human hearts, has become a human so that we may know the full extent of his love and that we may know and live in truth. Grace and truth came in Jesus Christ. There is no truth without grace, and God's truth is always personal, inviting, loving. And there is no grace without truth; God's truth is always what is best for us, the humans he created, and that he knows so well because he became one of us.

"I Tell You the Truth"

If truth is personal, then we as humans will come to know truth through a *personal* encounter with the personal God. That personal encounter is what God initiates. Jesus is alive and well, knocking on the door of every human heart (Rev. 3:20). Throughout the Gospel of John, Jesus repeats this phrase over and over: *"I tell you the truth."* Jesus tells us the truth we need to know, and it is full of grace and truth. Jesus doesn't force the truth on us; in love he woos us (John 6:44). But Jesus challenges us that if we just listen long enough, we will come to realize that what he says is exactly what we need: "*If anyone chooses to do my will, they will know whether what I say is true or not*" (John 7:17).

Jesus tells us that the world is full of lies about what is best for us, but he is trustworthy and speaks the truth. He came so that we may have life and have it to the full! (John 10:10). We can trust him because he is the one who lays down his life for us (John 10:14). Jesus tells us the truth that if we don't listen to him, we will "die" in the lies we listen to--life indeed will be meaningless (John 8:24). But through all the lies, we can hear the voice of Jesus, and if we will just listen to his voice and follow him, we will know the truth, and the truth will set us free (John 8:32). Truth is personal; Jesus says, "I am the Way, the Truth, and the Life" (John 14:6).

King Jesus is the Truth

After Pilate had introduced the bloody, beaten Jesus as the Human who reveals the Truth, a few minutes later he made an even more remarkable statement about this loving, suffering One: *"Behold, your King!"* (John 19:14).

God is full of grace and truth. As we listen to him, the truth will at first be offensive to us because it "contradicts us," it tells us in very personal ways how wrong our lives are. But God speaks truth to us only as the Crucified One. "Life in the truth begins at the point where it makes its uncompromising claim on us, not with the fist but with the defenselessness of the one who is 'the King crowned with thorns,' the Lamb upon the throne, yet nevertheless the King upon the throne."[1]

†

Thank you, Father God, that Truth matters because Truth gets played out in people's lives. I look at the world that doesn't believe there is Truth, and I see chaos. But I know that Truth matters, and I know that Truth is you, King Jesus. You have the authority to speak Truth into my life because you created me. You have the authority to speak Truth into my life because you suffered for me. You have the authority to speak Truth into my life because what you say is confirmed in the way people live and how they treat others. I surrender completely to your Truth because it is right, and it is filled with love. You, Lord Jesus, truly are the King, the only one that can make me human again. Praise your name!

---

[1]Eberhard Busch, *The Great Passion: An Introduction to Karl Barth's Theology* (Grand Rapids: Eerdmans, 2004), 136, quoting Karl Barth, *Church Dogmatics*, IV/3 450, 459.

FRIENDS ARE FRIENDS FOREVER

You learned it from Epaphras, our dear fellow servant, who is a faithful minister of Christ on our behalf, 8 and who also told us of your love in the Spirit. (1:7, 8)

What the people in Colossae *learned* was this explosive message of grace and truth. They learned that they were loved; that there was a larger story that made sense of reality and their lives; and that God was personally inviting them into this story of grace and truth. This was the "message of King Jesus," the Gospel that was changing lives all over the world. But learning about King Jesus involved both *hearing* the message and *seeing* the message. They needed assurance this message was true by seeing it played out in someone's life. And they saw the truth of the message in the life of the person who told it to them--Epaphras.

What did they see in the life of Epaphras that was different? Epaphras was a Gentile. He had not grown up with all the Jewish stories about a personal God. But this personal God reached out to him in love. He heard from Paul the story of Jesus, and then he felt the knock on the door of his heart by the risen Jesus, and everything changed. Paul had told him that the God of the universe was trustworthy, loyal, and faithful. Paul told him that this God proved that he could be trusted by emptying himself, coming down to be a human, loving us with extreme sacrificial love. Paul told Epaphras that God had powerfully confirmed the proof of his love through the resurrection of King Jesus from the dead. And then the risen Jesus began to work on Epaphras' heart in personal ways. God wasn't just "up there;" God began being "in here," inside Epaphras' heart and soul. The faithful, trustworthy love of God invaded Epaphras' life and he, too, became faithful, loyal, trustworthy, selfless, just like his Creator, King Jesus. Epaphras had become a changed man whose character was becoming like the character of King Jesus, and other people could see it. That was beautiful and attractive. People need to see the Gospel in our lives before they will listen to it. The Colossians first saw it in Epaphras, a faithful servant of people. Epaphras was changed because he had "Christ in him." And the love of God had invaded the lives of the Colossians because they too were changing to have that same loyal, faithful love of Jesus.

Paul says in Colossians 4:12 that Epaphras was always "wrestling" for the Colossians in prayer. The term "wrestling" (*agonizomenos*) is from the same root word that Paul will use to describe his own struggles on behalf of the Colossians (2:2), and we get our word *agony* from it. Every day, Epaphras would think about his friends in Colossae and spend time in his own spirit bringing them before the Spirit of God, asking God to mature them in their relationship with King Jesus. His love for the Colossians grew even stronger as he remembered them daily in prayer. There is something about praying for others that deepens your love for them. Maybe that's one reason Jesus told us to pray even for our enemies. They may not change, but as we pray, our attitude about our enemies will change. In turn, our relationship with them will change as we begin to think of them as friends instead of enemies. When that change begins in us, we can then imitate God and, in humility, seek reconciliation with them. Praying for others opens a whole new world of possibilities. Who in your life are you agonizing over in prayer? Keep praying; don't give up. God hasn't given up on you (and even now, Jesus is praying for you! — Rom. 8:34).

In the town of Colossae, Jesus was creating *a community of friends, friends who looked out for each other, called on each other, cared for each other.* This is the "love in the Spirit," the love of God helping us develop forever friends. "We need a community of friends. Friendship is not an added bonus to the Christian life, but is essential for following Jesus as the community of his disciples."[1] God meets our deep relational need for connection in a very real way—through the deep friendships he creates in his community of love.

†

God, thank you that even now, you watch and wait for me to turn to you every day. Father God, thank you that you "woo" me to you. Lord Jesus, just as you pray for me, today I pray for particular people in my life. I pray for those I love, and I also pray for those with whom I have a hard time getting along. I praise you that you can change relationships when I am willing to change. May those I am praying for today experience your goodness, presence, and love in their lives today. In the powerful name of the Spirit of our Lord Jesus, amen.

---

[1]Jeremy Treat, "Sexuality and the Church: How Pastoral Ministry Shapes a Theology of Sexuality," in *Beauty, Order, and Mystery: A Christian Vision of Human Sexuality*, Geral Heistand and Todd Wilson, eds. (Downers Grove, Il: IVP Academic, 2017), 53.

WALKING HABIT: BE A BETTER FRIEND

All of us desperately need *friends.* Friends we can see with our eyes; friends whose voice we hear and who take the time to listen. My Mom said the best way to have a friend is to be a friend. Ask God to bring a friend into your life, and ask God for the courage to step out and make friends. God created us to have friends, and in fact, God himself calls us his friends (Isaiah 41:8; John 15:13).

THE HOLY SPIRIT—"CHRIST IN YOU"

Epaphras also told us of your love in the Spirit. (1:8).

To [God's people] God has chosen to make known among the Gentiles the glorious riches of this mystery, which is Christ in you, the hope of glory. He is the one we proclaim, admonishing and teaching everyone with all wisdom so that we may present everyone fully mature in Christ. To this end, I strenuously contend with all the energy Christ so powerfully works in me. (1:27, 28).

Epaphras had told Paul and Timothy of the Colossians' "love in the Spirit." This is the only time in the book of Colossians where the Holy Spirit is explicitly mentioned. There are four other references in Colossians to the Spirit's activity (1:9, 1:11, 1:29, and 3:16). But interestingly, Paul's mention of the Holy Spirit in Colossians is minimal. Let that sink in for a minute. How can Paul, apostle and theologian par excellence, write four chapters with only giving brief mention to the Holy Spirit? Because Paul uses another description of the Holy Spirit's work throughout the book of Colossians, and it is the repeated phrase *"Christ in you."* In those places where Paul would normally speak of the Spirit's activity in our lives, he instead refers to King Jesus dwelling in us and working in our lives. Here's the point:

"Christ in you" and the Holy Spirit inside you are one and the same because what the Holy Spirit is doing is getting King Jesus inside you, filling you with the love of God in Jesus, changing you from one degree of glory to another to become more like the selfless King Jesus.

God the Spirit and God the Son (King Jesus) are so "One" that Paul will often refer to Jesus and the Spirit as one and the same: "the Spirit of Christ," "the Spirit of Jesus Christ," and "the Spirit of His Son" (Rom. 8:9; Phil. 1:19; Gal. 4:6). Paul says in Gal. 4:6 that because God has rescued us through Jesus, God has sent the *Spirit of His Son* into our hearts, the Spirit that calls out "*Abba!' (Daddy!),* Father." While there is much to unpack here, the following might help us begin to think about the Personal Presence of God in our hearts by His Spirit, who is "Christ in you, the hope of glory" (1:27). Or, as Paul prayed in Ephesians 3:16, may God "strengthen you with power through his Spirit in your inner being so that Christ may dwell in your hearts through faith."

1. *Jesus has brought a revolution in our understanding of God: God is a Community of Love*. Jesus has revealed to us that God is not some isolated, solitary Deity, but rather is a *community of self-giving love*: Father, Son, and Spirit. From all eternity, God has been full of love within himself, and he created us so that we could be independent creatures that can experience and enjoy that same love. Jesus taught and prayed this throughout John 13-17, summed up in this last verse: "I have made you known to them, and will continue to make you known, in order that the love you have for me may be in them, and that I myself may be in them" (John 17:26).

2. *Jesus the Son reveals the Father's Love*. God didn't just tell us facts about himself, he has shown himself as he really is

(a community of Father, Son and Spirit), and he has invited us into relationship with himself. There is no other "God." God is an extrovert, and the Son (and, as we will see, the Spirit too) is his "out-going," the very "radiance" of the Father. Jesus made it clear that his coming and all he did and taught was the expression of Father God: "*I and the Father are one. I do not speak of my own accord, but the Father who sent me commanded me what to say and how to say it. Whatever I say is just what the Father has told me to say. Anyone who has seen me has seen the Father.*" [1]

3. *The Spirit shines the spotlight on all that Jesus has done and is doing.* Just as Jesus has revealed exactly what Father God is like, the Spirit takes what Jesus has done and makes it real and understandable to us so that we experience God within our minds and emotions. Jesus says, "The Spirit of truth, who goes out from the Father, *will testify about me*. He will bring glory to me by taking from what is mine and making it known to you. All that belongs to the Father is mine. That is why I said the Spirit will take what is mine and make it known to you" (John 15:26; 16: 14, 15). The Spirit shines the spotlight on all that Jesus has done for us. The Spirit's work begins with our realization of all God has done for us (we are "rooted and grounded" in that love) and then matures us in his love so that our character becomes more and more like the character and heart of God, expressed so perfectly in Jesus his Son. "The Holy Spirit has no 'Face,' but it is through the Spirit that we see the Face of Christ, and in the Face of Christ we see the Face of the Father."[2]

---

[1]John 5:19, 20; 5:30; 7:16-18; 8:29; 10:17-18; 10:30; 12:49; 14:9, 10.
[2]Thomas F. Torrance, *The Christian Doctrine of God: One Being Three Persons* (London: T&T Clark, 2001), 63.

4. *Through the Spirit, we experience in our hearts the love of God.* The Holy Spirit, God's own Spirit and the Spirit of King Jesus, has "poured" God's love into our hearts (Rom. 5:5). The Spirit of God touches our hearts and emotions deep down, assuring us that God is a Father, and we are his children (Rom. 8:16). The Spirit in our hearts is a "down payment" or "deposit," guaranteeing what is to come forever (2 Cor. 1:22; Eph. 1:13).

5. *The Spirit of Jesus transforms our minds/identity/community/habits/character to become more like Jesus (God revealed to us).* In Jesus, we see the "face" of God, and the love of God penetrates our hearts and changes us from one degree of glory to another:

> *For God, who said, 'Let light shine out of darkness,' made his light shine in our hearts to give us the knowledge of the glory of God in the face of Christ....Now the Lord is the Spirit, and where the Spirit of the Lord is there is freedom. And we, who with unveiled face, all reflect the Lord's glory, are being transformed into his likeness with ever-increasing glory, which comes from the Lord, who is the Spirit (2 Cor. 4:6; 3:17,18).*

The Spirit transforms us as we cooperate with him by surrendering every aspect of ourselves over to his care: our minds, feelings, wills, bodies, and relationships. One of the most important ways the Spirit of King Jesus changes us is in our capacity to love. In our passage today, Paul is saying that the Spirit is the Source of such love. God's overflowing love grows into "fruit" that flows out of our lives into other people (Gal. 5:22-23).

✝

Father, Son, and Spirit—you are God, and you are my God! I praise you that you are a community of self-giving love. I praise you that even before you created the universe, you intended for us humans to be a part of and dwell in that community of love which is You. Spirit of God, thank you for pursuing me and piercing my heart with the incredible love shown so extravagantly in the crucified and risen Jesus. King Jesus and Spirit of God, make my heart your dwelling place. Clean up all the rooms, get rid of the dirty furniture, and open wide the windows to let your light disinfect me thoroughly. Furnish my heart with your truth, goodness, beauty, and love. I love you!

WHAT IS GOD'S WILL FOR YOUR LIFE? (PART 1)

For this reason, since the day we heard about you, we have not stopped praying for you. We continually ask God to fill you with the knowledge of his will through all the wisdom and understanding that the Spirit gives [all spiritual wisdom and understanding] so that you may live a life [walk] worthy of the Lord and please him in every way: bearing fruit in every good work, growing in the knowledge of God, being strengthened with all power according to his glorious might so that you may have great endurance and patience [with joy], and giving joyful thanks to the Father... (1:9-12)

With all wisdom and understanding he made known to us the mystery of his will, according to his good pleasure....I keep asking that the God and Father of our Lord Jesus Christ, the glorious Father, may give you the Spirit of wisdom and revelation, so that you may know him better. (Eph. 1:8-9, 17)

Have you ever wondered, "What is God's will for me?" We have so many decisions to make in our lives, some small and some extremely important (such as whom to marry, what vocation to go into, what job to take). What is God's will in all this?

That is a legitimate question, and God wants us to ask him for wisdom, counsel, and guidance. As James said, "If any of you lacks wisdom, you should ask God, who gives generously to all without finding fault, and it will be given you" (James 1:5).

For all of our specific decisions in life, we would be greatly helped if we could *first* understand God's "*Big Will*," what God really wants for us and our lives. That "Big Will" gives us discernment when we seek God's guidance on specific decisions we need to make. This passage gives us God's "Big Will." Let's look at that first, and then tomorrow we will explore how, in light of God's Big Will, we can seek God's guidance in our decision-making:

1. *God's Will is that we be Filled with the Knowledge of His Will.* Paul says that God's "Big Will" is that we be filled with the knowledge of God's will. But that sort of begs the question. What is "God's will"? Jesus gives us the answer in John 6:40: "For my Father's will is that everyone who looks to the Son and believes in him shall have eternal life (*zoe*, or quality life that is forever), and I will raise them up at the last day." Jesus also tells us what "eternal life" really is: "This is eternal life: that they *know you*, the only true God, and Jesus Christ, whom you have sent" (Jn. 17:3). The "will of God" is that we *know* him and let his love invade our lives and transform us forever. This "knowledge" of God is much deeper than just knowing there is a God. The Hebrew word for knowledge, *yada*, connotes intimate knowledge, even that of a husband and wife (Gen. 4:1). This is the kind of intimate, relational knowledge God desires. Paul puts it well in Ephesians, praying that we "being rooted and grounded in love, may have power, together with God's people, to grasp how wide, long, high, deep is the love of Christ, and to know this love which surpasses knowledge,

that you may be filled to the full with all the full measure of God" (Eph. 3:19).

The Greek word Paul uses for knowledge in verses 9 and 10 (*epignosis*) is not just "knowledge" (which would be *gnosis*), but rather "full" knowledge [(*epi* ("full") *gnosis* ("knowledge")]. God wants you to get the "Big" picture of everything he has done for you in Jesus, and not just for you, but for the entire world. God wants to "fill you," but not just with information about God. We don't just come to "know about" God; we come to "know" God in a relational way, just like you know your best friend. This is relational knowledge: we learn about God's character by trusting him, and the more we grow in relationship with him, we trust him deeper for everything in our lives. As in any relationship, God comes to know us, too (see Gal. 4:8). The interesting thing is that as we open up to him and let him know us, we actually learn so much more about ourselves than we ever knew before.

Knowledge of God *experiential, relational, participatory.* It is like the knowledge we received from our parents when we were young, or from a beloved mentor who loved us and taught us. It is like an apprenticeship, and Jesus is our Master Teacher. This God-given experiential knowledge (given by his Spirit) completely transforms the way we live our lives and understand the world. God's "full knowledge" gives us "a comprehensive vision of truth—cosmic and human, spiritual and material, divine and mundane—whose focal point is [Christ]."[1] God wants you to know exactly what his "Big Will" is for your life, which is to rescue you in every way and fill your life with love, peace, joy, Spiritual wisdom and understanding, community, hope—fruit that will last.

---

[1]John M.G. Barclay, *Colossians and Philemon* (Sheffield: Sheffield Academic, 1997), 77.

2. *God Wants to Fill us with all Spiritual Wisdom and Understanding*. This "full knowledge" comes about through both "wisdom" (*sophia*) and "understanding" (*sunesis*) that the Spirit of God gives. The book of Proverbs describes how "wisdom" and "understanding" are the secrets to living a full, joyful life. Proverbs says that true wisdom and understanding begin with trusting that God's ways are pleasing and perfect and that God freely gives wisdom and understanding to all who seek it: "The reverence/acknowledgement of God is the beginning of wisdom…For the Lord gives wisdom, and from his mouth come knowledge and understanding" (Prov. 1:7, 2:6). We, as Christians, now have access to the complete wisdom and understanding from God, the full answer to all that God has always intended for the world. This wisdom and knowledge come to us in the relationship we have with God through King Jesus: "So that you may have the full riches of complete understanding, in order that you may know the mystery of God, namely King Jesus, in whom are hidden all the treasures of wisdom [*sophia*] and understanding [*sunesis*] (2:2,3)." Let's explore what "wisdom" and "understanding" mean:

- *Wisdom.* Wisdom is different than having information or data. Our world is filled with information but little wisdom. Wisdom is being able to understand what all the information *means*. Wisdom is discerning, seeking to apply to one's life and to other's lives those things that are enduring and lasting. Wisdom looks for the bigger picture and tries to discern the long-term impact of any decision. Wisdom means we bring our decisions humbly before God and ask him for discernment.

- *Understanding*. The Greek term *sunesis* literally means "bring together," and it implies the God-given ability to

> take God's wisdom and apply it to any given situation which may arise in life.[2] As N.T. Wright notes, "wisdom" is mental excellence in general, and "understanding" is the ability to think through a subject coherently and clearly.[3] Understanding is practical knowledge.

We should be assured that God wants to fill us with his "full knowledge" in King Jesus (experiential knowledge of God and a comprehensive vision of the world), his "wisdom" so that we can make wise decisions with a worthy goal in mind, and the understanding to bring it all together and think coherently about our decisions. Tomorrow, we will get practical and see how God's "Big Will" can help us in all our decision-making.

†

Father God, thank you that your will is that I may know you in an ever-deepening, relational way; to know your heart, your love, and your good plans for my life, family, and loved ones. I humble myself before you, acknowledging that wisdom and understanding comes from you. I offer up myself and my plans to you today. Thank you.

---

[2]See William Barclay, *The Letters to the Philippians, Colossians, and Thessalonians* (Philadelphia: Westminster Press, 1975), 108.
[3]Wright, *Colossians*, 61.

WHAT IS GOD'S WILL FOR YOUR LIFE? (PART 2)

> *For this reason, since the day we heard about you, we have not stopped praying for you. We continually ask God to fill you with the knowledge of his will through all the wisdom and understanding that the Spirit gives [all spiritual wisdom and understanding] so that you may live a life [walk] worthy of the Lord and please him in every way: bearing fruit in every good work, growing in the knowledge of God, being strengthened with all power according to his glorious might so that you may have great endurance and patience [with joy], and giving joyful thanks to the Father... (1:9-12)*

> *With all wisdom and understanding, he made known to us the mystery of his will, according to his good pleasure.... I keep asking that the God and Father of our Lord Jesus Christ, the glorious Father, may give you the Spirit of wisdom and revelation, so that you may know him better. (Eph. 1:8-9, 17)*

We saw previously that God wants us to know his "Big Will" for our lives, which is to have experiential (relationship) knowledge of God, letting his love invade our hearts and rescue us from every destructive thing (including, and especially, ourselves). This ever-deepening relationship with God will bring into our hearts and minds love, joy, peace, Spiritual wisdom and understanding, community, and hope. Through this ever-deepening relationship with God, God will give us spiritual wisdom and understanding to help us make wise decisions and live mature lives. Let's look today at how knowing God's "Big Will" helps us in our decision-making.

Paul says God gives us full knowledge and Spiritual wisdom and understanding so that we may "live a life worthy of the Lord and may please him in every way, *bearing fruit* in what we do and growing more and more in knowledge (*gnosis*) so that we may have *great endurance and patience, joyfully giving thanks to God.*" In other words, our knowledge of God is not just "head knowledge," but it begins to affect and transform every area of our lives. What Paul identifies here also helps us when it comes to making decisions. In every decision we face, we should ask, "What is the outcome of my decision?"

Specifically, based on what Paul says in these verses, we should ask:

- Does this please God and *bear fruit*? Is my decision going to positively or negatively impact someone else? Is it helping me become more of the human God created me to be?
- In the decision I make, am I taking the easy way out, or the more fruit-bearing way that will give me endurance, patience, and character (the "fruits of the Spirit")?
- Does this lead to deeper joy and a more thankful life?

Putting all this together, and in light of God's "Big Will," how can I discern God's wisdom in making specific decisions? When seeking God's wisdom in making a decision in our lives, one important thing to remember is that God has dignified us by allowing us to be the ones to decide. Often, we hear that

God has a "specific will" about exactly what we should do in any given situation, as if there is some "bullseye" and if we miss that "bullseye," we have missed the will of God. But the Bible doesn't teach that. As Carry Friesen and Robin Maxson note in *Decision Making and the Will of God*, "in those areas where the Bible gives no command or principle, the believer is free and responsible to choose his own course of action. Any decision made within the moral will of God is acceptable to God."[1] There may be a number of "good options" in front of us, and God has dignified us by allowing us to make responsible decisions. But in making our decisions, we certainly can and should ask God for wisdom (James 1:5).

Like a good Father, God wants us to mature in how we make decisions. The Bible is replete with help in this regard, and here are some questions gleaned from Scripture that will help in making wise, God-honoring decisions:

- What Biblical principles should inform my decision?
- Do I have all the facts?
- Have I sought the advice of wise counselors?
- Are my motivations pure and God-honoring? Have I asked God to reveal what is in my heart, what is driving my thinking in making this decision?
- Am I rushing into this decision too quickly? Should I step back and take more time?
- Am I honestly considering any warning signs?

[1]Carry Friesen with J. Robin Maxson, *Decision Making and the Will of God: A Biblical Alternative to the Traditional View* (Portland, Oregon: Multnomah, 1980), 179.

- What are the possible outcomes of this decision, and will they lead me further into God's "Big Will" for my life?[2]

†

Father God, Lord Jesus, Spirit of wisdom and truth, I thank you for the peace you give me in every situation. I don't need to be fearful because you are with me, and you hold my right hand. Continue to help me understand your "Big Will" for my life, to continue to learn the full knowledge of what you have done and are continuing to do in this world. I pray for wisdom to take a long view and perspective about my life and my decisions. Give me understanding to bring together all the various factors in my decision-making, and give me your peace to trust you when I can't yet see the way forward. I bring before you the specific decisions I am facing now. Let me listen to you through your Word and through wise counselors. I lay my requests before you and wait in expectation.

---

[2]For an excellent discussion, see Blake Holmes, "Ten Biblical Principles for Decision Making," May 7, 2019, at https://www.watermark.org/blog/decision-making-principles. See also these Biblical principles for decision-making: Prov. 1:7, 11:14, 12:15, 13:20, 15:22, 19:2, 19:20, 21:5, 22:3; Psalm 25:8-9, 32:8; James 1:19-25, 3:17,18.

HOW TO MATURE IN DISCERNING GOD'S WILL

For this reason, since the day we heard about you, we have not stopped praying for you. We continually ask God to fill you with the knowledge of his will through all the wisdom and understanding that the Spirit gives [all spiritual wisdom and understanding] so that you may live a life [walk] worthy of the Lord and please him in every way: bearing fruit in every good work, growing in the knowledge of God, being strengthened with all power according to his glorious might so that you may have great endurance and patience [with joy], and giving joyful thanks to the Father, who has qualified you to share in the inheritance of his holy people [the saints] in the kingdom of light. (1:9-12)

As we discussed previously, God's "Big Will" is that we be infused with God's full knowledge and Spiritual wisdom and understanding. How does the Spirit of King Jesus infuse us with these? It won't happen automatically. Remember, this is a relationship, so we have to participate if this relationship is going to deepen. So how does God infuse us with full knowledge, wisdom, and understanding?

God transforms us by the renewing of our minds. The full knowledge, wisdom, and understanding that God gives includes our emotions, bodies, will, and relationships. But it begins with our *minds; it doesn't end with our minds, but it begins with our minds.* Throughout the Old Testament, God called people to listen to his Word: "Come, let us reason together," "The Word is not far off, but it is near you;" "Listen to his voice, for the Lord is your life!" (Isa. 1:18; Deut. 30:11-14; 30:20). Jesus told us that the greatest commandment ("greatest" because it is the one that is the "greatest" for us) is to love God with all of our minds as well as our heart, soul, and strength (Mark 12:30). Paul stresses repeatedly that spiritual transformation begins with our minds:

> *Don't be conformed to the world's ways, but be transformed by the renewing of your minds. Then you will be able to experience God's good, pleasing and perfect will. (Rom. 12:2)*
>
> *Those who live according to the flesh have their minds set on what the flesh desires. Those who live by the Spirit have their minds set on what the Spirit desires. The mind of the flesh is death, but the mind controlled by the Spirit is life and peace. (Rom. 8:6).*
>
> *You have put off the old self and have put on the new self, which is being renewed in knowledge in the image of its Creator. (Col. 3:10)*
>
> "For Christians to 'grow up' in every way will include the awakening of intellectual powers, the ability to think coherently and practically about God and his purposes for his people."[1]

---

[1]Wright, *Colossians,* 62.

Our brains change through what we think about. Thinking about God, his love and his ways will also physically change our brains, providing much needed "mental health." One of the most important and exciting scientific discoveries over the last twenty years is how we can actually change the neuropathways in our brains by what we think about and by what we habitually do. As Dr. Timothy Jennings writes in *The God-Shaped Brain: How Changing Your View of God Transforms Your Life*:

> Recent brain research at the University of Pennsylvania has documented that all forms of contemplative meditation were associated with positive brain changes—but the greatest improvements occurred when participants meditated specifically on a God of love. Such meditation was associated with growth in the prefrontal cortex (the part of the brain right behind our forehead where we reason, make judgments and experience Godlike love) and subsequent increased capacity for empathy, sympathy, compassion and altruism….Not only does other-centered love increase when we worship a God of love, but sharp thinking and memory improve as well. In other words, worshipping a God of love actually stimulates the brain to heal and grow.[2]

Knowledge of God is experiential knowledge, leading to fruitful lives. God doesn't give us information about himself; he gives us *himself.* The "knowledge" that God brings is an experiential knowledge, a knowledge that makes sense of ourselves, our lives, and the universe. This experiential knowledge grows over time, making us more certain of the Reality and Love of

[2]Jennings, 27. See also Andrew Newberg and Mark Robert Waldman, *How God Changes Your Brain: Breakthrough Findings from a Leading Neuroscientist* (New York: Random House, 2009); John Medina, *Brain Rules* (Seattle: Pear, 2008).

God because he has been walking with us the entire way. Our lives become a "spiral upward," as we increase in this experiential knowledge, which will change us to become the people we want to become. "Understanding will fuel holiness; holiness will deepen understanding."[3] Jesus promised that, from heaven, he would continue to make God known to us as we live in him, and he lives in us: "I have made you known and will continue to make you known in order that the love you have for me may be in them and that I myself may be in them" (Jn. 17:26)

God makes Himself known by empowering us for patient endurance. Because knowledge of God is experiential, God will "empower us" (*dunamoumenos*) with the strength we need for daily living, and especially when life is difficult. Paul says that as we make room for God in our hearts and minds, he will strengthen us "with all power according to his glorious might so that you may have patient endurance." Paul makes a similar statement in 1:29 when he says that he is able to continue his ministry even through difficulty because of "all the energy (*dunamis)* he so powerfully works in me." You can trust that when you need the Personal Presence of God, when you need patience to endure, he will supernaturally fill you with his comfort and strength: "The Lord is near. Do not be anxious about anything, but in everything, by prayer and petition, with thanksgiving, present your requests to God. And the peace of God, which transcends all understanding, will guard your hearts and minds in Christ Jesus" (Phil. 4:5-7).

†

Father God, you have my attention. I praise you for making me whole; you give me the peace I desperately

---

[3]Wright, *Colossians*, 62.

need. Thank you for your Word, upon which I meditate, and which changes my whole outlook on life. Jesus, thank you for meeting me today through your Spirit and your Word, giving me encouragement and patient endurance. I turn over to you now my anxious thoughts in exchange for your peace. Thank you, Almighty God and my Father.

THE NEW EXODUS

Giving joyful thanks to the Father, who has qualified you to share in the inheritance *of his holy people [the saints] in the kingdom of light. For he has rescued us from the dominion of darkness and brought us into the kingdom of the Son he loves, in whom we have redemption, the forgiveness of sins. (1:12-14)*

God raised us up with Christ and seated us with him in the heavenly realms in Christ Jesus, in order that in the coming ages he might show the incomparable riches of his grace expressed in his kindness to us in Christ Jesus. (Eph. 2:6)

Paul and the early Christians realized (through the leading of the Spirit) that in Jesus, a new "exodus" has occurred. The exodus of the people of Israel from Egyptian slavery and death demonstrated the love and the power of Yahweh. But it was also a foreshadowing of an even greater exodus, not just for the people of Israel but for all humanity; not just from political oppression but from slavery to our selfishness and past; and not just from a culture of death but from death itself and the fear and meaninglessness of death. These two verses are jam packed with images and metaphors taken from the Old Testament, which find their fulfillment in what Jesus has done. Let's unpack them:

1. *Just as God rescued the nation of Israel from Egypt, God has now rescued us from the death culture of our world.* Just as God sent Moses into the far country of Egypt to rescue, bring back, and exalt the people of Israel, God has sent His Son into the far country of this world to rescue us, to restore our humanity, and to *exalt humans* to become like the Son, the prototype of humanity. God did not abandon humanity or this earth—God never abandons anything. He "redeems" broken things, restoring and healing us. He does this through forgiveness. Forgiveness is our "exodus" from our broken past into a new, healed future. A few verses later (1:22), Paul will describe this redemption and forgiveness as God "reconciling" us back to him. "Reconciliation" (*katallasso*) literally means to "exchange," and that is exactly what God has done in Jesus. As Karl Barth notes, God humbled himself in exchange for humanity's exaltation. Barth says that God is the "prodigal" by going into the "far country" and becoming man in the second Person of the Trinity (the Son or the Word). And then Jesus returns home to God as the "Son of Man," bringing with him our redeemed humanity, our true humanity: "It was God who went into the far country, and it is man who returns home. Both took place in the one Jesus Christ."[1]

2. *We are beginning to enjoy now the inheritance of the First-born Son.* In the Old Testament, the Jews were the "holy people" and the "children" of God. And just like the first-born son in Old Testament times, the children of Israel received an "inheritance" which included being the people of God, receiving a "kingdom" with God as their king and protector, and receiving a place to live and flourish in the land of Canaan (see Ex. 6:6ff). But God's intention in choosing

[1]Karth Barth, *Church Dogmatics*, IV.2, 20.

Israel was that the whole world would be blessed (Gen. 12:2,3; Isa. 42:6,7), and Jesus is the culmination and fulfillment of Israel. Jesus is the "Firstborn" Son of God, but instead of hoarding his inheritance, he shares all the treasures and love of God with people of every nation, tribe, and tongue. King Jesus has rescued us from slavery and the death-dealing ways of the world and has brought us into his Kingdom and his protection, and now all people the world over have the right to become the precious children of God (Jn. 1:12,13). This Kingdom is not just something we will someday enjoy in heaven. King Jesus has rescued us *now* and transferred us *now* into his Kingdom, and through his Spirit we are enjoying *now* a down payment of all that we will enjoy forever (2 Cor. 1:22; Eph. 1:13,14). God has rescued us and seated us with him *now*, far above all rule and authority in this age and in the one to come (Eph. 1:20, 21).

> God's future has arrived in the present in the person of Jesus, summoning everybody to become people of the future, people in Christ, people remade in the present to share the life of God's future.[2]

†

Almighty God, the God who fights for people. Thank you for traveling to the far country of this world to rescue us from the darkness and death in this world, and for transferring us to your kingdom of light. King Jesus, thank you for taking hold of me and never letting me go, and for pulling me up and sitting me now in your care and protection, far above all the dark powers in my

---

[2]N.T. Wright, *Surprised by Hope: Rethinking Heaven, the Resurrection, and the Mission of the Church* (New York: HarperOne, 2008), 287.

world. I rest in you now, and praise you that nothing will ever separate me from your love.

HEAVEN BEGINS NOW

> *Giving joyful thanks to the Father, who has qualified you to share in the inheritance of his holy people [the saints] in the kingdom of light. For he has rescued us from the dominion of darkness and brought us into the kingdom of the Son he loves, in whom we have redemption, the forgiveness of sins. (1:12-14)*

> *God raised us up with Christ and seated us with him in the heavenly realms in Christ Jesus, in order that in the coming ages he might show the incomparable riches of his grace expressed in his kindness to us in Christ Jesus. (Eph. 2:6)*

In these verses from Colossians and Ephesians, Paul is saying that King Jesus has transferred us *now* into his Kingdom and has already seated us in the "heavenly realms." What does he mean? The sense here is that "heaven" is invading our present. While God has promised the "age to come" with a new earth united with heaven (where there is no brokenness), we need to feel the force of the New Testament teaching that in Jesus the "age to come" has broken into and is transforming this world *now*. In fact, *Jesus changes everything we thought about heaven and earth.*

Unfortunately, Christians have developed a very un-Biblical understanding of what God has done in Jesus as it relates to heaven, and verses like our reading today from Colossians and Ephesians give us a much-needed correction. N.T. Wright lays out well the "un-Biblical" understanding and then the thorough Christian understanding:[1]

The Un-Biblical Understanding of Christianity and Heaven

1. The goal is the final bliss of heaven, away from this life of space, time, and matter, or as Wendall Berry describes, "incanting anemic souls into heaven."[2]

2. This goal is achieved for us through the death and resurrection of Jesus, which we cling to by faith.

3. Christian living in the present consists of anticipating the disembodied, "eternal" state through the practice of a detached spirituality and the avoidance of "worldly" contamination.

The Biblical, Christ-Centered Understanding of Christianity and Heaven

In contrast to the above, the Bible teaches the following:

---

[1]See N.T. Wright, "Why Christian Character Matters," in James K.A. Smith and Michael L. Gulker, eds., *All Things Hold Together in Christ: A Conversation on Faith, Science, and Virtue* (Grand Rapids: Baker Academic, 2018), 184-185.

[2]Wendall Berry, "Christianity and the Survival of Creation," in *Sex, Economy, Freedom, and Community* (New York: Pantheon, 1992), 114.

1. The goal is a new heaven and new earth, with *embodied* human beings raised from the dead to be the renewed world's rulers and priests.

2. This goal is achieved through the kingdom-establishing work of Jesus and the Spirit, which we grasp by faith, participate in by baptism, and live out in love.

3. Christian living in the present consists of anticipating this ultimate reality through the Spirit-led, habit-forming, truly human practices of faith, hope, and love, sustaining Christians in their calling to worship God and reflect his glory into the world.

The reason Christians live differently is not because we are trying to gain some "prize" in heaven someday. The reason Christians live differently is because *this is the way life is supposed to be lived.* The "prize" is beginning now as we learn that we don't have to live the way the world lives. King Jesus has come to us (just like Moses went into Egypt) and has rescued us now from the death-dealing ways of this world. We are thankful that God has awakened us and is teaching and training us "in advance the language of God's new world."[3] N.T. Wright does a masterful job of helping us understand heaven and the Kingdom of God in *Surprised by Hope: Rethinking Heaven, the Resurrection, and the Mission of the Church.* As he writes:

> The whole point of what Jesus was up to was that he was doing, close up, in the present, what he was promising long-term, in the future. And what he was promising for that future, and doing in the present, was not saving souls for a disembodied eternity but rescuing people from the corruption and decay of the way the

[3]Wright, "Why Christian Character Matters," 186.

> world presently is so that they could enjoy, already in the present, that renewal of creation which is God's ultimate purpose—and so they could become colleagues and partners in that larger project.[4]

Paul's and Timothy's description of how Jesus has transferred us now into his Kingdom is a prelude to what they will say next. These next few verses, which we will explore in the coming days, are the most explosive and eye-popping words ever written. They unveil the mystery of all of reality, the "hidden in plain sight" key to unlocking the mystery of humanity, the goal of us and of all reality.

†

Father God and King Jesus, I praise you that you have come into the far country of this world. You have rescued me, breaking all the chains of selfishness and fear that hold me down. You have freed me and brought me now into your Kingdom, into the sphere of love, freedom, and protection. We don't yet see the world or ourselves as we shall be, but we see Jesus, the pioneer, prototype, and prelude of what will be forever. I love your Kingdom, Jesus! Thank you for rescuing me and seating me now with you, far above all rule and authority, for there is no rule or authority, no reality, greater than you!

---

[4]Wright, *Surprised by Hope*, 192.

HYMN TO THE HIGH KING

Father God has rescued us from the dominion of darkness and transferred us into the Kingdom of the Son he loves,

Who is the image of the invisible God,

The firstborn over all creation;

For in him all things were created

things in heaven and on earth, the visible and invisible, whether thrones or powers, whether rulers or authorities.

All things were created through him and for him.

He is before all things, and in him all things hold together.

He is the head of the body, the church.

Who is the beginning,

the firstborn from the dead, so that in everything he might have the supremacy.

For in him all God's fullness was pleased to dwell.

And through him to reconcile all things to himself, whether things on earth or in heaven,

By making peace through his blood, shed on the cross. (1:13-20)

These verses read like a poem or a song. Most scholars believe it was a hymn to Jesus sung by early Christians (a similar hymn is found in Phil. 2:5-11). This hymn is the center of Colossians; everything revolves around this praise to King Jesus. You could even say the hymn is the center of the entire Bible, maybe the most profound words ever written. In these verses, Paul makes the boldest, most audacious claims about this Jesus of Nazareth. At the core of the Christian message is the deep security that every last atom and molecule in this far-flung universe, from the Pleiades and Orion down to your little self, was created by God the Son, whom we have come to know through Jesus of Nazareth. Everything was also created *for Jesus:* the reason everything was created was to display the amazing love of God for humans revealed in Jesus--the love that created and now recreates human beings.

The hymn is divided into two parts: how all of creation was created by and for the Son of God, and now how all of creation is recreated and made new through the Son of God and his body, the church of Jesus. Each part of this beautiful hymn emphasizes how Jesus, the Son of God, is King of the Universe. And *God did all this for you!* The Creator God is not some far off, unknown deity. The hands that fashioned you in your mother's womb have nail scars on them. The Creator God who crafted your miraculous body slipped into a human body himself, emptying himself just for you, came down and took hold of you, rescuing you from the powers that oppress you, and is pulling you up to become the human he had created you to be in the first place. These verses are explosive because they boldly assert just how much God is *for you!*

I urge you to take 5 minutes every day for the next 30 days to read or listen to Col. 1:15-23. Let it penetrate the depths of your soul so that you will be rooted and grounded in the love of King Jesus. Let this message dwell in you richly. Paul has just said that God has taken us out of the sphere of the world of meaninglessness, fear, and hate, and has brought us into the sphere of his love, the sphere controlled by Jesus, the Word of God to us. We are now safely in the sphere of Jesus; we are now in his loving arms and fear-releasing Presence.

A Hymn for Today

The hymn captures our imaginations, providing a comprehensive worldview. In their book, *Colossians Remixed*, Brian J. Walsh and Sylvia C. Keesmaat (a husband and wife team) note that *images* are so much more important in our culture than substance, and marketers and politicians know it. The way political parties, business enterprises, or social movements achieve any level of influence or power is through our *imaginations*. Unfortunately, we are inundated by images—every day, every minute, there is some new image, new fad, new technology, new product. The constant barrage has dulled our imaginations. We are jaded because we know that most of these images are thrown at us from ulterior motives--to make a buck off of us, get our vote, or achieve some level of power or control. Old Testament scholar Walter Brueggemann rightly notes that

> …the key pathology of our time, which seduces us all, is the reduction of the imagination so that we are too numbed, satiated and co-opted to do serious imaginative work.[1]

---

[1] Walter Brueggemann, *Interpretation and Obedience* (Minneapolis: Fortress, 1991), 199.

Walsh and Keesmaat argue that one way to set us free from the dulling imagination of our cultural empires is "to write evocative and subversive poetry that provides an imagination alternative to the empire's."[2] Walsh and Keesmaat do this by taking Paul's beautiful hymn to King Jesus and adapting it to our current cultural situation. Below is a portion of their adaptation of the hymn to King Jesus for our times:[3]

In an image saturated world,
a world in which the empire of global economic affluence
has achieved the monopoly of our imaginations,
in this world
Christ is the image of the invisible God
In this world, Driven by images with a vengeance
Christ is the image par excellence
The image above all other images
The image that is not a façade
The image that is not trying to sell you something
The image that refuses to co-opt you.
Christ is the image of the invisible God
A flesh and blood
Here and now
In time and history
With joys and sorrows
Image of who God is.
Image of who we are called to be
Image bearers of this God.
He is the source of a liberated imagination.
A subversion of the empire

---

[2]Brian J. Walsh and Sylvia C. Keesmaat, *Colossians Remixed: Subverting the Empire* (Downers Grove, Il: IVP Academic, 2004), 85.
[3]The full beautiful poem can be found at Walsh and Keesmaat, 85-89.

Because it all starts with him
And it all ends with him.
Everything
All things
Whatever you can imagine
Visible and invisible
Mountains and atoms
Outer space, urban space and cyberspace
Whether it be the Pentagon, Disneyland, Microsoft or AT&T
All things have been created in him and through him
He is their source, their purpose, their goal
Even in their rebellion
Even in their idolatry
Their power and authority is derived at best
Parasitic at worst
In the face of a disconnected world
Where home is a domain in cyberspace
Where neighborhood is a chat room
Where public space is a shopping mall
Where information and technology promise a tuned-in, reconnected world
All things hold together in Christ
The creation of a deeply personal cosmos
All cohering and interconnected in Jesus.

†

King Jesus, you are worthy of all praise, adoration, and love! Thank you that finally, in you, my life has purpose. You are the beautiful purpose of all reality. Everything was created by you, and everything was created to enjoy and display your limitless love. Everything, including my life, is held together by your nail-scared hands. You have purchased me with your sacrificial love, and your love fills me with joy. Praise you, my High King!

IMAGO DEI

> *Who [the Son] is the image of the invisible God, the firstborn over all creation. For in him all things were created: things in heaven and on earth, visible and invisible, whether thrones or powers or rulers or authorities; all things have been created through him and for him. He is before all things, and in him all things hold together. (1:15-17)*

The hymn to King Jesus is about *creation* and *new creation.* God the Son, embodied and revealed in the human Jesus, is the one who created everything, and Jesus, God with us, is the one who recreates everything. "The God who made the world in Christ will redeem it through Christ, for God has not abandoned the cosmos and its inhabitants."[1] Let's look today and tomorrow at *who Jesus is* and what he has done in *creation.* Then we will look at *who Jesus is* and what he has done and is doing in *re-creation*, and how Jesus is beginning to re-create the world through his body, the church.

Jesus is the Image of the Invisible God and the Creator of Everything. This man, Jesus of Nazareth, crucified but raised from the dead, is the physical "image" (*eikon*) of the invisible God. The great Creator God of the universe is *Spirit.* God transcends space, time, and matter and is active everywhere *as*

[1]Thompson, 28.

Spirit all the time. But Jesus reveals to us, in our own flesh and blood humanity, exactly what this Spirit God is like. Echoes of this thought are found in other places in the New Testament (particularly John 1 and Hebrews 1): *No one has seen God; God the only-begotten Son has made him known; The Son is the radiance of God's glory and the exact representation of his being.*[2] In space and time, at just the right time in human history, God became one of us to achieve his cosmic purposes. God is not incomprehensible; he has made himself known through the people of Israel and in the human Jesus, the fulfillment and culmination of Israel's purpose. God revealed himself in a human face, and that face is Jesus (2 Cor. 4:6).

Paul goes even further in this passage to say that *everything* (you, me, and even all the "powers") was created in and through Jesus, the Son. The "Word" through which God spoke the universe into existence was the Son, the Word of God (Jn. 1:1). Paul is probably also alluding to the Jewish concept that Wisdom was the "firstborn" of creation and was involved in creating everything (Proverbs 3:19, Proverbs 8, and the Apocryphal books of Sirach and Wisdom). The Jews came to believe that "Torah is the instrument of creation…and serves to instruct God's people, mediating knowledge of him and his ways."[3] But as Paul will say, all the wisdom and knowledge of God are found in Jesus, and Jesus is the fulfillment of the Torah.

> He [Jesus] encompasses the function of Torah within himself. He is the greater reality, and creation and revelation take place through and in him. For Christ is, in fact, the one to whom Torah alludes when it speaks of God creating the world.[4]

---

[2]John 1:18, Hebrews 1:3.
[3]Thompson, 115.
[4]Id.

Humans are Created in the Image of God. Jesus is the "image of God" (Latin, *imago Dei*). But the Bible also says humans are created in the "image of God" (Gen. 1:26-28). How can we understand these two concepts, and what is their connection? Before we explore the beautiful connection between them (which we will do tomorrow), let's first explore *what it means to say that humans are created in the "image of God."*

Genesis tells us that God made humans, male and female, in his "image" (Hebrew *tselem*) and "likeness" (Hebrew *demut*) (Gen. 1:26-28). Interestingly, the Bible uses these same words to describe idols. An idol was a little statute made of wood or stone that "represented" a false god. These little statutes were more than just wood or stone: "an idol was a manifestation of divine presence in the world."[5] Against this background, Genesis uses these terms "as a declaration that God intended to create human persons to be the physical means through which he would manifest his own divine presence in the world."[6] Thus, after creating humans, God told them (both male and female) to cultivate the earth and subdue it (Gen. 1:26-28). As Old Testament scholar John Walton notes, one aspect of God creating us in his image is that "we serve as his substitute by representing his presence in the world...This is part of the human role—to serve as vice regents for God in continuing the process of bringing order [to the world]."[7] *Created in the image of God means to reflect and represent God in his created universe.*

What else does the Bible say about us being created in the "image of God?"

[5]Marc Cortez, *Resourcing Theological Anthropology: A Constructive Account of Humanity in the Light of Christ* (Grand Rapids, MI: Zondervan, 2017), 109.
[6]Id.
[7]John H. Walton, *The Lost World of Adam and Eve: Genesis 2-3 and the Human Origins Debate* (Downers Grove, IL: IVP Academic, 2015), 42.

- *All* humans are created in the image of God. It is this quality about humans that gives every person dignity and worth, and this idea is the very basis of Western civilization. Being created in the image of God "is specifically affirmed of males and females and is nowhere limited by age, race, social class, or any abilities. As an image-bearer of God, every human being inherently possesses dignity."[8]
- Created in the image of God means we are intended *to be in relationship with God.* God's intention has always been to "dwell" with the humans he created and to have a love relationship with us. That is why we humans feel fully alive when we are in relationship with God—we are fulfilling our human vocation when we love God with all our heart, soul, mind, and strength. *Created in the image of God means to have a connection with God.*
- But our relationship with God is not a private affair; our relationship with God allows us to have full, vibrant relationships with others. God said, "Let *us* make mankind in *our* image;" God is a community of love, and he created humans to also be in community. In fact, "humans" are not just male and not just female; God created humans "male and female" in the image of God. This "unity in diversity" reflects the image of God. "Thus, human beings cannot image God fully apart from an 'in-dependence-upon-one-another' relationship. We are not free *from* others, but rather free *for* others."[9] *Created in the image of God means we are intended to be in relationship with others. To be human is to have a relationship with God that flows into relationships with other humans.*

---

[8]John S. Hammett and Katie J. McCoy, *Humanity* (Brentwood, TN: B&H Academic, 2023), 80.
[9]Hammett and McCoy, 100.

- Created in the image of God is not dependent on our physical or mental abilities. God, who is Spirit, is able to connect in spirit with all humans regardless of their physical or mental abilities. Every human has a spirit. As Hammett and McCoy note, "those suffering some disability of their rational capacities may still be able to experience relationship with God on another level…In spirit, we deal with something that all humans possess equally as an aspect of the human constitution."[10]
- Humanity's turn from God (the "Fall") has *not* taken away our bearing the "image" of God (see particularly Gen. 9:6, Jas. 3:9). What humans have lost is the "glory" that God intended for humans. While God had created us to be his representatives in this world (to cultivate and subdue it), we have certainly made a mess of things. But God has never, ever given up on humans, nor does he intend to. And that is where the real story begins (as we will see tomorrow).

These are some ways in which humans are created in the image of God. But Paul says that Jesus is the true and unique "image of God," and Paul makes the beautiful (and critical) connection between Jesus as the image of God and humans as bearing the image of God. How can we understand this beautiful connection? We will explore this tomorrow.

†

Creator God, it is amazing to think that you created me in your image and likeness. I am fearfully and wonderfully made! You have endowed me and every human in this world with eternal dignity and worth. Help me to

---

[10]Hammett and McCoy, 117.

remember that in every person I see or talk to today. King Jesus, I praise you that you have come to restore the glory that you created us to have, an eternal glory that is just beginning. Thank you, Father God and King Jesus, for creating me and for recreating me to become all you intended me to be, to the praise of your glorious grace. Amen!

GOD CREATED AND RECREATES US IN HIS IMAGE

Who [the Son] is the image of the invisible God, the firstborn over all creation. For in him all things were created: things in heaven and on earth, visible and invisible, whether thrones or powers or rulers or authorities; all things have been created through him and for him. He is before all things, and in him all things hold together. (1:15-17)

The god of this age has blinded the minds of unbelievers so they cannot see the light of the good news of the glory of King Jesus, who is the image of God. For God, who said, 'Let light shine out of darkness,' made his light shine in our hearts to give us the light of the knowledge of the glory of God in the face of King Jesus. (2 Cor. 4:4, 6)

God created every one of us in his "image," which endows every person with dignity and worth. And yet, Jesus uniquely reflects the "image of God." How can we understand this, and what does this mean for us?

Jesus is the true Image of God and the prototype for humanity. Paul says that Jesus is the "firstborn" over and above all creation. The Greek word for "firstborn" is *prototokos*, or "prototype." Another word for "prototype" is "blueprint." Humans were in a sense patterned after Jesus—Jesus is the blueprint. *Jesus reveals perfectly what humans were created to be*. When we read the Gospels, we see how humans are supposed to be, connected with God and reflecting his character. We see God's divine Presence expressed through Jesus' selflessness, humility, compassion, truthfulness, and dependence on God.

Jesus is the reason God created the universe. Even before he created the universe, God intended for humans to be like Jesus (see Rom. 8:29; Eph. 1:14): "the Son himself is God's eternal idea of what a true human should be."[1] Paul and Timothy even say in this passage that God created everything for this exact purpose—all things were created "in Jesus" and "*for Jesus*." All things were created to display the incredible love of God and to show us what it means to be humans created in the image of God. "Christ is the *purpose* or *goal* for which God created the world. The creation of the world already anticipates its ultimate goal, its perfection. This includes the perfection of humankind, since the new humanity found in Christ is humanity as it was created to be."[2]

Jesus enables us to become the humans God originally created us to be. More than Jesus just being a "model" or "example" for us to look at, Jesus recreates us through his Spirit in us to become like him, the humanity God created us to be. In Jesus, we see that God has not abandoned his human creation, but has come down to us as a human to *recreate us*. "Humanity was made as the climax of the first creation; the true humanity of Jesus is the climax of the history of creation, and at the same

---

[1]Cortez, 124.
[2]Thompson, 116.

time the starting point of the new creation."[3] Jesus is both the *standard* and the *enabler* of who God created us to be.[4]

The early church fathers pictured it this way: to be created in the image of God means we "mirror" or reflect God. But in turning to other "gods" (and in becoming our own "gods"), the mirror has become tarnished and covered with dirt. Jesus, the perfect reflection of God, clears the dirt and restores the image. Athanasius put it beautifully that Jesus is both the *artist*, recreating the image in us, and the *model* "according to which the image in each of us is made, the model who has come to dwell in this world, the Creator's art studio."[5]

Jesus, the artist, is now recreating us to become the humans God created us to be through his Spirit and through renewed relationships in the church (his body). As we saw previously, "Christ in me" and the Holy Spirit in us are referring to the same, powerful energy that God works inside our hearts and minds. "The power behind the image restoration is that of the Holy Spirit. The Holy Spirit is part of our personal renewal as redeemed humanity, effectuating the work of Christ in our earthly lives and being the guarantee of our future perfection (Eph. 1:13,14)."[6] This is a progressive change that occurs in us as we allow every part of ourself (mind, body, soul, relationships) to be changed by the love of God. "Now, in Christ, the living out of God's intention in creating humans in his image is progressively being realized in believers in renewal and transformation, and will one day lead to complete conformity to the

---

[3]Wright, *Colossians,* 74.
[4]John F. Kilner, *Dignity and Destiny: Humanity in the Image of God* (Grand Rapids, MI: Eerdmans, 2015), 233.
[5]Nonna Verna Harrison, *God's Many-Splendored Image: Theological Anthropology for Christian Formation* (Grand Rapids, MI: Baker, 2010), 40, referencing Athanasius, *On the Incarnation* 14:1-2.
[6]Hammett and McCoy, 86.

image of Christ."[7] We will explore practical ways this happens as we read the rest of Colossians, our pamphlet for how God can make us human again.

John Kilner summarizes well what it means to be recreated in the image of Jesus, the image of God:

> Ultimately, the image of God is Jesus Christ. People are first created and later renewed according to that image. Image involves connection and reflection. Creation in God's image entails a special connection with God and an intended reflection of God. Renewal in God's image entails a more intimate connection with God through Christ and an increasingly actual reflection of God in Christ, to God's glory. This connection with God is the basis of human dignity. This reflection of God is the beauty of human destiny. All of humanity participates in human dignity. All of humanity is offered human destiny, though only some embrace and will experience it. Christ and humanity, connection and reflection, dignity and destiny—these lie at the heart of what God's image is all about.[8]

†

Father God and King Jesus, thank you for giving me dignity and worth by creating me in your image. Thank you for giving that same dignity and worth to every person, and help me to remember that today as I interact with people. We are thankful that you have not given up on our sad, selfish, fearful world, but you are constantly pursuing us to redeem us to become all that you had

---

[7]Hammett and McCoy, 89.
[8]Kilner, xi.

originally created us to be. We are so thankful that you have the power and the love to recreate us to become glorious creatures, renewed according to the knowledge of King Jesus, who truly reflects who you are. And we praise you that our complete recreation is guaranteed through the resurrection of Jesus from the dead, and our bodies will be like his glorious body. Praise your Name!

KING JESUS IS RE–CREATOR THROUGH THE CHURCH

> *He is the head of the body, the church; he is the beginning and the firstborn from among the dead, so that in everything he might have the supremacy. (1:18)*

> *And God placed all things under his feet and appointed him to be head over everything for the church, 23 which is his body, the fullness of him who fills everything in every way. (Eph. 1:22,23)*

We now move from creation to re-creation, from what Jesus has accomplished for us to what he is accomplishing now *in us* and how he is doing it. The scope is awe-inspiring, but the means are very human, gritty, down to earth, and all with you in mind.

Paul has just described with majestic language how everything in the universe was made by King Jesus--to display the powerful love of God. And now, all of a sudden, he brings up the *church!*

Many non-believers will say that while Jesus is attractive, they can't believe in him because of the church. Yet Jesus won't allow that alternative. Jesus has so aligned himself with the community he loves that Paul calls the church "his body." Sure, there are hypocrites in the church, but the real truth is that *everybody* is a hypocrite (if we will just admit it). And the church is exactly the place where we can admit it-- where all our faults can come out in the open, and we can be healed by love and be changed by Jesus.

The Church is Essential to Becoming Human Again. The church is not an option because in God's plan, human beings are not an option. The church is the place where humans come into the sphere of God's love and begin to be renewed according to the image of Jesus, humanity's Creator. "The church of which Jesus is the head is humanity as it was created to be."[1] The church is crucial to what God is doing in Jesus because God created us in his image, and God himself is a *community* (Father, Son, and Spirit). *We cannot become fully human without being with other people.* God is a community, and he created humans to be within a community, and the church is the place where God restores our humanity through community. For both Jesus and Paul, *church is essential to becoming human again.* Paul says that God placed everything in all creation under Jesus "*for the church*, which is his body, the fullness of him who fills everything in every way" (Eph. 1:22, 23). For Paul, "participation in the local community was essential to the process of maturation, such that the local church is both the place where and the means through which maturation occurs."[2] The church displays to all creation the multifaceted wisdom of

---

[1]Thompson, 33.

[2]James G. Samra, *Being Conformed to Christ in Community: A Study in Maturity, Maturation and the Local Church in the Undisputed Pauline Epistles* (London: T&T Clark, 2006), 135, quoted in Humanity, 261.

God, bringing people from all ethnic groups together to become the renewed people of God (Eph. 3:10, 11).[3]

Jesus is the Head of a New Humanity. The word "head" (*kephale*) can mean "source" as well as the one who provides right "direction." In these verses, Paul and Timothy are saying that Jesus is the source of this new humanity, the church, and we become human again as we are nourished by his love, direction, and wisdom. If we lose connection with the "head"—Jesus--we will drift into all sorts of destructive ways of thinking. The body image Paul uses also highlights the organic nature of the church. The church is not an organization or hierarchy. It is a community of servants, and the greatest is the one who serves. Jesus is our model, and he has taught us that his power is found by living sacrificially for others. The church is not only the body of Jesus, it is also the "family of God," creating bonds and relationships even closer than blood relatives (Eph. 3:15). The church is where a new humanity is being formed, a family closer than blood, committed to each other and learning to love the way Jesus has loved us.

Jesus Recreates Humanity through the Church. Return with me to Walsh's and Keesmaat's modern day adaptation of the Hymn to the High King, which now emphasizes the beauty of the body of Christ:

In a "show me" culture where words alone don't cut it
The church is
The flesh and blood
Here and now

---

[3]Some excellent resources to check out on "church" are Dietrich Bonhoeffer, *Life Together* (New York: Harper, 1954); Collin Hansen and Jonathan Leeman, *Rediscover Church: Why the Body of Christ is Essential* (Wheaton, IL: Crossway Books, 2021); and Irwyn L. Ince, Jr., *The Beautiful Community: Unity, Diversity, and the Church at its Best* (Downers Grove, IL: InterVarsity Press, 2020).

In time and history
With joys and sorrows
Embodiment of this Christ
As a body politic
Around a common meal
In alternative economic practices
In radical service to the most vulnerable
In refusal of the empire
In love of this creation
The church reimagines the world
In the image of the invisible God.
In the face of a culture of death
A world of killing fields
A world of the walking dead
Christ is at the head of the resurrection parade
Transforming our tears of betrayal into tears of joy
Giving us dancing shoes for the resurrection party.
And this glittering Joker
Who has danced in the dragon's jaws of death
Now dances with a dance that is full
Of nothing less than the fullness of God
This is the dance of the new creation
And in this dance all that was broken
All that was estranged
All that was alienated
All that was dislocated and disconnected
What once was hurt
What once was friction
Is reconciled
Comes home
Is healed
And is made whole
Because Grace makes beauty out of ugly things

And it all happens on a cross
It all happens through blood
Not through a power grab
It all happens in embraced pain
For the sake of others
It all happens on a cross
Arms outstretched in embrace
And this is the image of the invisible God
This is the body of Christ.[4]

†

Lord Jesus, thank you for creating me as a person who needs other people. Thank you for the people in my life. Thank you for creating the church, a community of broken people saved by your mercy whose bond is the love of God. Thank you for teaching us how to love others better through being in this community of loved ones. Help me to take whatever next steps I need to take to become more deeply committed to a body of Jesus believers. Thank you that you have shown us that the joy of loving others is a thousand times worth the risk. Thank you, Lord Jesus, that your body is the place where broken people are reconciled, come home, and are being healed.

[4]Walsh and Keesmaat, 87-89.

JESUS IS KING OF THE WORLD

He is before all things, and in him all things hold together. 18 And he is the head of the body, the church; he is the beginning and the firstborn from among the dead, so that in everything he might have the supremacy. (1:17, 18)

Jesus has the authority and the ability to recreate humanity and to create the new community, the church, because of the cross and the resurrection. Paul uses three titles to emphasize this:

Jesus is the Beginning. Paul's term here is *arche*, which means beginning but also means "source," "creative initiative," and "power."[1] He has overcome the hateful "powers" by his sacrificial love for humanity, and he has disarmed their power of fear and oppression. How has he proven that he is more powerful? By his resurrection from the dead. God has brought the *power of the future age into the present* in the resurrection of Jesus, "in order that the power of the new age might be unleashed upon the world while there was still time for the world to be saved."[2]

Jesus is the Firstborn over Death. Paul uses the term *prototokos* again (prototype), but this time he is not referring to Jesus as the prototype of humans in creation, but the prototype of

[1]Wright, *Colossians,* 78.
[2]Wright, *Colossians,* 79.

humans for re-creation, for eternity. Jesus is the *first* to overcome death, but he is not the last. Because he rose from the dead, death is not going to be the end of you, either! Jesus is the "first fruit" of those who will overcome death (1 Cor. 15:20). His resurrection guarantees not only that God is more powerful than death, but that God's love will not let death separate us from him (Rom. 8:38, 39). Just as Jesus now has a *glorious, spiritual body* (but a body nonetheless), so we shall also be clothed with a glorious, spiritual body like Jesus. As Paul said, "Just as we have borne the image of the earthly human, so shall we bear the image of the heavenly human" (1 Cor. 15:49).

Jesus is the World's True Lord and King. Paul uses one more title here to describe Jesus: he is the "Preeminent One" (the *proteuon*). Scot McKnight believes Paul is using this word as a title:

> Here we come face to face with the gospel itself, which is more than a message of salvation: the gospel is the declaration that Jesus of Nazareth, who lived, who died, and who is risen to the right hand of the Father, is the world's true Lord and King. The gospel announces that Jesus is Proteuon![3]

To sum it up, Jesus has begun to recreate humanity so that we may become the people that God, through Jesus the Son, had initially created us to be. The church (people rescued, redeemed, and being changed by grace) are that new humanity whom Jesus will not let go. He has gripped us so tightly by his love that we are part of his own body. As the life source of his community, Jesus nourishes us with his love and wisdom, and in this community we learn how to love others and how to live life to the full. We live in the confidence of his love because no

[3]McKnight, 159.

power in the universe, including death, is any match for King Jesus. He is the creative beginning of the age to come, and he has proven this in his resurrection. His resurrection is the beginning of all the resurrections to come (yours and mine), and his sacrificial love for you and his powerful triumph over evil and death prove indeed that he is the true Lord and King of this world, forever!

> *King Jesus, you are worthy of all our praise and adoration because you were slain, and with your blood, you purchased for God persons from every tribe and language and people and nation. You have made them to be a kingdom and priests to serve our God, and they will reign on the earth. (Rev. 5:9, 10). Praise your Name!*

THE REASONS GOD CAME

For God was pleased to have all his fullness dwell in him, 20 and through him to reconcile to himself all things, whether things on earth or things in heaven, by making peace through his blood, shed on the cross. 21 Once you were alienated from God and were enemies in your minds because of your evil behavior [hostile in mind, doing evil deeds]. 22 But now he has reconciled you by Christ's physical body through death to present you holy in his sight, without blemish and free from accusation— 23 if you continue in your faith, established and firm, and do not move from the hope held out in the gospel. This is the gospel that you heard and that has been proclaimed to every creature under heaven [in all creation], and of which I, Paul, have become a servant. (1:19-23)

In these power-packed verses, Paul follows the Hymn to the High King by giving the reasons why King Jesus is the Source, the Firstborn from the dead, the Preeminent One, and the Head of his body, the church. The first word in this verse, "for," can be translated "because," and these verses explain why Jesus created us and is now recreating us.

Why did God do it? Paul highlights four reasons why King Jesus came:

It pleased God to have all his fullness dwell in Jesus so that all the fullness of God might also dwell in us. Paul emphasizes in Colossians that all of God's "fullness" (*pleroma*) is in the man Jesus: "in King Jesus all the fullness of the Deity lives in bodily form" (Col. 2:9). Just as the Spirit of God filled the tabernacle and moved with the people of Israel as they journeyed in the wilderness to the promised land, so in one man in time and space, the man Jesus, God has "tabernacled" with us human beings. The Word that created the world became flesh and tabernacled/dwelt with us (Jn. 1:14). No one has seen God, but God the Son in the man Jesus has made him known (Jn. 1:18). Jesus prays, "I have made you known to them, and will continue to make you known, in order that the love you have for me may be in them and that I myself may be in them" (Jn. 17:26).

Paul says that while all the "fullness" of God dwells in bodily form (in Jesus' humanity as well as now by his presence in his body, the church), we who are "in King Jesus" have also been brought to fullness in him (Col. 2:9). What is this "fullness" that God is giving us in Jesus? The fullness is God himself—love, joy, peace, patience, kindness, goodness, gentleness, faithfulness, self-control. Paul prays that we "being rooted and established in love, may have power, together with all God's holy people, to grasp how wide and long and high and deep is the love of King Jesus, and to know this love which surpasses knowledge—that you may be *filled to the full measure of all the fullness of God*" (Eph. 3:18, 19).

It pleased God to reach out in reconciliation to an angry and hostile world. Often, we think God is the one who is hostile and is somehow out to judge and harm us. But we have it completely backwards! *We* are the ones who are hostile and angry with God because we don't know him. It is our own minds and selfish attitudes that make us hostile, and even enemies, with

God. As Paul says, "Once you were alienated from God and were enemies in your minds because of your evil behavior" (Col. 1:24). But God is the one who takes the initiative to make peace with us, to end our hostility with God. God has done everything he can to make peace with us, and in his eyes, we are already reconciled to him. In King Jesus, God was reconciling the world to himself, not counting any of our faults (even the worst) against us (2 Cor. 5:19). As Paul urged, "Be reconciled to God!" (2 Cor. 5:20).

How has God effected this reconciliation? By taking all the fault himself and letting evil do its worst on him. In these verses, Paul hints at a theme that runs throughout Colossians: in the cross of Jesus, God has exhausted all the "powers" of the evil one and has taken away all the power of evil to accuse us of wrongdoing. By his great reconciling love, we are "without blemish and free from any accusation." If God is for us, no one can condemn us (Rom. 8:31).

Walsh and Keesmaat remind us of just how relevant the cross is to the "powers" that hold us down:

> All the ways the empire of death held you captive and robbed you of your life—the exhausting and insatiable imperative to consume, the bewildering cacophony of voices calling out to us in the postmodern carnival, the disorientation and moral paralysis of radical pluralism, the loss of self in a multiphrenic culture…the struggle not to become roadkill on the information highway—all of this is nailed to the cross, and you are set free. Let's not beat around the bush here. What is at stake in this conflict at the cross is indeed a power struggle…In this power struggle, sacrificial love is victorious pre-

> cisely by being poured out on a cross, a symbol of imperial violence and control.[1]

It pleased God to suffer with and for us to free us from all hostile powers. Paul says *all things* were created by the Son to display the love of God through the Son. That includes all "powers" that try to destroy us and hold us down. The very things that make us afraid, disillusioned, bitter, and anxious were created by Jesus, but they (like us) have turned away from God and toward their own selfish ends. But they now have zero power. Any power they have is derived power, and Jesus has disarmed their power to harm us in any way. God has done this through reaching out to us, stooping to make us great, taking all of the evil upon himself in the cross.

> On the cross, God's power is disclosed not in its undeniable capacity to destroy or as reluctant to forgive, but rather as the self-giving power to heal and renew, to bring wholeness to the world created in Christ. God's power is not grasping and manipulative, but giving and serving. God's power further empowers people to live in ways commensurate with a God who discloses power in such ways.[2]

It pleased God to restore all of creation and nature. When God restores humanity to himself, he is also restoring all of nature. In Jesus, God is reconciling "all things, whether things on earth or things in heaven." When God created us, he gave us the freedom to choose for or against him, but in his mercy, he placed limits on our destructiveness, which includes death. Because of this, all of creation "groans" for new creation (Rom. 8:22). As Paul says in Romans 8:19ff, "For the creation waits

---

[1]Walsh and Keesmaat, 137-38.
[2]Thompson, 117.

in eager expectation for the children of God to be revealed. For the creation was subjected to frustration, not by its own choice, but by the will of the one who subjected it, in hope that the creation itself will be liberated from its bondage to decay and brought into the freedom and glory of the children of God." As Ted Peters reminds us, "we cannot separate human destiny from cosmic destiny. What happens to persons depends on what happens to the cosmos."[3] But the miraculous resurrection of Jesus is the sign of an ultimate cosmic transformation. All the universe itself will be recreated when humans are finally transformed and provided new, but very physical, glorified bodies. As the physicist John Polkinghorne writes,

> The resurrection of Jesus is the seminal event from which the whole of God's new creation has already begun to grow. God's total creative intent is seen to be intrinsically a two-step process: first the old creation, allowed to explore and realize its potentiality at some metaphysical distance from its Creator; then the redeemed new creation which, through the Cosmic Christ, is brought into a freely embraced and intimate relationship with the life of God.[4]

Paul closes this passage with a bold statement: the gospel of King Jesus "has been proclaimed to every creature under heaven." How are we to understand that, when we know that there are people even in our world today who have never heard of Jesus? As Wright notes, Paul is saying that what God has done through King Jesus permeates all of creation and will eventually be restored and recreated because of Jesus:

---

[3]Ted Peters, *God--The World's Future: Systematic Theology for a New Era* (Minneapolis: Fortress, 2000), 327.

[4]John Polkinghorne, *The God of Hope and the End of the World* (New Haven: Yale University Press, 2002), 113, 116.

From whales to waterfalls, the whole created order has in principle been reconciled to God. Like a sovereign making a proclamation and sending off his heralds to bear it to the distant corners of his empire, God has in Jesus Christ proclaimed once and for all that the world which he has made has been reconciled to him.[5]

†

Thank you, God Almighty, for reaching out in reconciling love. Thank you, that I am secure in your power and love, and I do not need to be afraid of anything in my life. You have defeated and disarmed the powers that cause me fear. You have not given us a spirit of fear but the Spirit of power, love, and self-control. Thank you, God, that your purposes will be accomplished and neither death nor any power can separate us from your love.

---

[5]Wright, *Colossians,* 89, 90.

HOW JESUS STILL SUFFERS FOR PEOPLE (AND HOW YOU CAN JOIN IN)

> *Now I rejoice in what I am suffering for you, and I fill up in my flesh what is still lacking in regard to Christ's afflictions, for the sake of his body, which is the church. 25 I have become its servant by the commission God gave me to present to you the word of God in its fullness— 26 the mystery that has been kept hidden for ages and generations, but is now disclosed to the Lord's people. (1:24-26)*

Paul is one of those heralds announcing the Good News that in Jesus Christ God has reconciled all of creation to himself (1:23-26). Paul's life was transformed by this Good News. Paul went from seeking his worth in achievement and "self-righteousness" to being in love with the God revealed in King Jesus. The love of God became his driving energy, comfort, rest, hope, and source of life. His life ambition could be summed up in this question: "*How is my life accomplishing what God is doing through Jesus?*"

Paul and Timothy are writing the Colossian letter from a prison cell, either from Rome or most likely from Ephesus. They are in jail because they are Christians who are vocal about their faith. Paul once put Christians *into* jail, but after meeting the risen Jesus, his life was filled with jail time. And not only jail time, but a lot of discomforts that most people would do anything to avoid. As he put it, five times he was flogged by the Jews, three times beaten with rods, once pelted with stones, three times shipwrecked (spending a day and a night in the open sea), and constantly in danger of his life (see 2 Cor. 11:23-29). And yet, Paul was the most joyous person you would ever meet. As he wrote from a Roman prison cell to the church in Philippi, "Rejoice in the Lord! I'll say it again: Rejoice!" (Phil. 4:4). Paul had exchanged a life of comfort, prestige, fame, maybe even early retirement, and had joined the Jesus adventure, an adventure in loving people with the love of God. Such a life will invariably require serving and suffering.

Paul and Timothy write that they are now in a jail cell on behalf of the church in Colossae. Similarly, in Ephesians 3:1, Paul says that he is a prisoner of the Lord for the sake of the Gentiles. These are truthful statements because unless Paul was vocal about Jesus, the good news would never have arrived in Colossae, although Paul's preaching had also landed him in jail. But then Paul says something which at first blush is difficult to understand: "I fill up in my flesh what is still lacking in regard to King Jesus' afflictions, for the sake of his body, the church." What does Paul mean here? What could be lacking in Christ's sufferings on the cross?

Let's first answer this by saying that in the sense of what saves us as human beings, absolutely *nothing* is lacking in what God has done for us on the cross. God himself suffered for us on the cross, taking upon himself all the blame for our evil. God certainly doesn't need anybody else to do anything for him—we can't add to God's amazing love. As Paul would say in Ephesians, because of God's great love for us, we are saved solely by his grace (Eph. 2:4,5). So what does Paul mean?

To answer this, remember when the risen Jesus appeared to Paul on the road to Damascus? What did Jesus say? "Saul, Saul, why are you persecuting *me*?" (Acts 9:4). Paul wasn't persecuting the risen and ascended Jesus. Or was he? Yes, he was persecuting Jesus because Jesus was saying that he is so closely aligned with us, his people, that when we hurt, Jesus hurts. Remember what Jesus said in the parable of the sheep and the goats: "When you failed to do it to one of the least of these, you failed to do it to me" (Matt. 25:45). Jesus still suffers with humans, and that is what Paul means in these verses. Jesus is still suffering for and with humans everywhere. Jesus is still ministering the world over—his Spirit groans with us as we groan (Rom. 8:26). God aches that all people might come to know his love and that his Kingdom would put an end to the unnecessary suffering and evil in the world. What Paul is doing is joining Jesus in the continual suffering that Jesus still suffers for others.

Paul's whole view of his life—his life's goal—had become so aligned with Jesus that he would view everything he did, every new project or phase in life, with this question in mind: *"How is this accomplishing what Jesus is still suffering to bring about in the world?"*

If we want to get in on the greatest adventure of our lives (and the greatest thing we could ever do in this world and in the age to come), we will join King Jesus in what he is doing. But we need to know that this will inevitably involve suffering of some sort. All of us will face some sort of suffering in this life, whether we are Christians or not. But King Jesus completely changes how we suffer and the meaning of suffering. God suffers with us, and the cross proves that. The Spirit of this suffering God, the Father of all compassion, comforts us in all our sufferings (2 Cor. 1:3,4). God never abandons us in our suffering, but joins us, and he can even turn our suffering into something good instead of meaninglessness (Rom. 8:28). As Paul would say, "We are hard-pressed on every side, but not crushed; perplexed, but not in despair; persecuted, but not abandoned; struck down, but not destroyed…we do not lose heart. Though outwardly we are wasting away, yet inwardly we are being renewed day by day. For our light and momentary troubles are achieving for us an eternal glory that far outweighs them all" (2 Cor. 4:8, 9, 16, 17).

†

Thank you, God, for teaching me how to love. Thank you for filling my life with purpose and meaning and calling me to join you in serving other people. Thank you for breaking me out of my shell of selfishness and fear. Help me today to notice people in my life who need you. Help me to more clearly view everything I am doing through the lens of "How is this accomplishing what Jesus is still suffering to bring about in this world?"

THE GREATEST OF ALL MYSTERIES

> *I have become its servant by the commission God gave me to present to you the word of God in its fullness — 26 the mystery that has been kept hidden for ages and generations, but is now disclosed to the Lord's people. 27 To them God has chosen to make known among the Gentiles the glorious riches of this mystery, which is Christ in you, the hope of glory. (1:25-27)*

Do you like a good mystery? I love mysteries. I love trying to figure out who did it and how they did it. The twists, the turns, the surprise endings. The best mystery writers are those who sprinkle clues throughout the story and then at the end there is the "Aha!" moment when you say "Of course! It was right there all along, but I missed it!"

God is mysterious because he is beyond our comprehension. And God loves mysteries, too. The way God has interacted within history is full of surprises. For example, take the tiny, helpless nation of Israel. Although God works through mighty nations and "big" things, he has worked particularly through this ancient, small group of people, not because they were large or great, but exactly because they were small (Deut. 7:7). And in the history of Israel (which God preserved so that we could all see how God works), God would often save the best for last in people's lives. Like Sarah and Abraham, finally blessed with a baby long after child-bearing years. Like David, the youngest in the family, the one you would least expect to be chosen to be the future king. But of all the unlikely things God has ever done, what about God loving humans so much that he became one? And what about God rescuing humans through a suffering, crucified King? As Paul would say, "the foolishness of God is wiser than human wisdom and the weakness of God is stronger than human strength" (1 Cor. 1:25).

People are mysterious, too. Why is humanity so great one minute and so destructive the next? What is the "mystery" of life, the mystery that will help us learn to live better, to love better, to flourish and live fruitful lives?

Sprinkled throughout the history of the world, and particularly the history of the Jews, are clues to the greatest of all mysteries. This mystery is also the mystery that answers the riddle of humanity, the answer to the question, "What does it mean to be human?" This mystery of God is the secret to everything. Here is this mystery, the answer to the riddle of humanity:

"The mystery is King Jesus in you, the hope of glory."

Let's explore this mystery of King Jesus:

- First, King Jesus is a mystery that God had hinted at in all his dealings with the Jews, but he had kept hidden "for ages and generations" (1:25; Rom. 16:25). When Paul uses the term "mystery," he doesn't mean something that is hard to understand, but rather something that had been under cover in the past but is now fully disclosed.
- All of the Old Testament foreshadowed Jesus, and all that God intended has now been "fully revealed" in Jesus. The mystery of what God planned from even before the creation of the world, he has now revealed fully and completely in Jesus (1 Cor. 2:7; Eph. 1:4). Jesus displays per-

fectly God's original intention in creating the world, as well as how God is recreating the world.

- The mystery *is King Jesus*--the crucified, risen, and now ruling one. To the world, this seems strange—a crucified, rejected, humiliated teacher is how God saves the world from itself? But that is exactly how God rescues us, and the history of the world since Jesus proves how effective God's mysterious strategy is. King Jesus is humanity's hope of glory. In other words, God has unlocked the mystery of humanity, he has revealed exactly how humanity can escape its self-destruction. Jesus has, in the words of Revelation, "opened the scroll" that is the destiny of humankind and revealed how the world will be saved from destroying itself (Rev. 5:1-6). "Christians believe that not only the mystery of the divine, but also the deepest truths about human life and destiny, have been revealed in Jesus Christ."[1]

- This is the "secret" to the universe itself. But this "secret mystery" is not a concept, idea, or doctrine. The mystery is King Jesus himself (2:2,3). The God who created the amazing universe is indeed a mystery. But God has taken away the mystery of God and made himself known to us on our level, with a human face.

- God has not just made himself known in Jesus; he has made himself "fully" known. There is no other God behind or instead of Jesus; everything we need to know about God is fully disclosed in King Jesus. There is also no other "philosophy" that comes close to matching the profound

[1]Mary Catherin Hilkert, "Cry Beloved Image: Rethinking the Image of God," in *In the Embrace of God: Feminist Approaches to Theological Anthropology*, ed. Ann Elizabeth O'Hara Graff (Maryknoll, NY: Orbis, 1995), 201.

yet simple wisdom in Christianity. As Paul and Timothy said, in Jesus are found all the treasures of wisdom and knowledge (2:2,3).

- King Jesus has brought to each one of us the nearness of God—God wants to dwell within each of us. As God's Spirit and "glory" (Hebrew, *kabod*) flooded the tabernacle and temple, now God's glory dwells with us, physically in the man Jesus of Nazareth, and now in our hearts, minds, souls, and very being through the Spirit of the risen Jesus.
- Although every human being still bears the "image of God" and sin has not taken that away, every human has fallen short of the "glory" of God (Rom. 3:23). But God is restoring that glory—Jesus is the "hope of glory." As we spend time in the presence of Jesus, we come to know God; we come to know who he is, his character, and we especially come to experience his great love for us. As we spend time in the presence of Jesus, "we are being transformed into his image from one degree of glory to another" (2 Cor. 3:18).
- When Paul says, "Christ in you," the "you" is *plural*. Paul means that Jesus is in each of us, but also that King Jesus is in us as we are together with others, as we are in his community, the church, his body. God never intended for us to be alone, and only when we are in a community with others can we come to know God more fully. "The local church is both *the place where* and the *means through which*" we know God more fully and become more like King Jesus.[2]

---

[2]James G. Samra, *Being Conformed to Christ in Community: A Study in Maturity, Maturation and the Local Church in the Undisputed Pauline Epistles* (London: T&T Clark, 2006), 135, quoted in Humanity, 261.

†

Creator God, you are a mystery! How can I ever comprehend you? I cannot unless you make yourself known. Thank you for coming near and making yourself known in a way I can understand—with a human face. You made yourself known in such a way that I can understand who I am, why I am here, where I am going. But even more, you make yourself known through the Spirit of Jesus, invading my heart, mind, soul, and spirit, dwelling within me, and changing me to become all that I so deeply desire. You, Creator God, Father, Word of God, Spirit of Love and Truth, are accomplishing your perfect will to love and remake me like Jesus. I love you!

THE GOAL OF COLOSSIANS

He is the one we proclaim, admonishing and teaching everyone with all wisdom, so that we may present everyone fully mature in Christ. 29 To this end, I strenuously contend with all the energy Christ so powerfully works in me. (1:28, 29)

The mystery that is now fully revealed to everyone the world over, the mystery that solves the riddle of humanity, is not a philosophy, dogma, or set of principles. It is a *person*—King Jesus himself. Everything about Christianity has its center and focus on Jesus. Christianity strays from itself and ventures into aimless, even destructive, teachings when Jesus is not the center. Jesus comes first; everything else in our thinking and teaching will fall beautifully in line when he is first and center. As McKnight says,

> The gospel message is first about Jesus and only then about salvation. It is a mistake to think the gospel can be reduced to the message of our salvation; the gospel is the message about Christ who is King, Lord and Savior. The gospel saves because the Messiah is the Savior; the Savior is not the means of the gospel but its content.[1]

---

[1]McKnight, 198, 199.

The letters of Paul always deal with some sort of distortion of Christianity in one way or another, and Colossians is no exception. And the reason for these distortions was because the churches he was writing to were taking their focus off Jesus. As we will see later in the letter, there were some who were telling the Colossians that what they really needed were mystical experiences, and they could obtain these through following a regimented discipline program (2:18-23). Paul says, "they have lost connection with the head [Jesus], from whom the whole body, supported and held together by its ligaments and sinews, grows as God causes it to grow" (2:19). Paul's whole goal in ministry, and the goal of the letter to the Colossians, is to help people mature in their growth in Jesus: "so that we may present everyone fully mature in Christ" (see also Eph. 4:13).

Paul mentions three things we should keep in mind about maturing in Jesus:

1. *The Goal is maturity in King Jesus, not perfection.* Paul uses the word *teleion,* which means the end or the goal, and "mature" is a good way to understand it. Christians often use the word "sanctification" (meaning "becoming holy") to describe the process of spiritual growth, but "maturity" might be a more understandable term for us today. What God wants to do is to make us more *mature*--more able to deal with the difficulties in our lives in a responsible, loving manner. That end or goal is to become more like Jesus. Heaven is not our goal; heaven is our destination. Our goal is to conform to the image of Jesus, to become more like Jesus in every way (Rom. 8:29). This does not mean perfection, but it does mean constantly moving toward that goal of maturity in Jesus. As Paul said in Philippians "I want to be found in [Jesus], I want to know Christ...Not that I have already obtained all this, or arrived at my goal, but I press on

to take hold of that for which Christ Jesus took hold of me" (Phil. 3:9, 10, 12).

2. *Maturity in King Jesus requires right thinking*. Paul says that his ministry involves both "admonishing" and "teaching." The word for admonishing (*nouthetontes*) involves correcting or setting straight. Part of Christian maturity is making sure we correctly understand what we believe, and this is especially true in our Internet age with so much false information and teaching available. As Mark Twain said, "What gets us into trouble is not what we don't know. It's what we know for sure that just ain't so." N.T. Wright says that "part of the task of one who proclaims Christ is to straighten out confusions, to search for and tie together correctly the loose ends of half-grasped ideas, so that the positive teaching may not be instantly distorted upon reception, but may be properly understood, appreciated and lived out."[2] For us as Christians, that *always* means coming back to Jesus as the center and *always* grounding what we believe in Scripture. As Walsh and Keesmaat describe, "The point is to so immerse ourselves in the Scriptures, so indwell their narrative, be so permeated by their images, that our imagination is transformed according to the image of Christ."[3]

3. *Christian maturity comes as King Jesus dwells within us.* Paul finishes these verses by saying that he works toward that goal of helping others mature in Christ "with all the energy (*dunamis,* or "dynamite") that Christ so powerfully works within me." Paul had come a long way from a self-righteous Pharisee focused on his "goodness" and "image" to a selfless, loving, mature person. How did that come

---

[2]Wright, *Colossians*, 97.
[3]Walsh and Keesmaat, 85.

about? Jesus did it. Jesus did it when Paul took his focus off himself and fell in love with God. He fell in love with the God revealed in Jesus. He fell in love with God when he understood how compassionately and extravagantly God loves all of us. When you realize you are loved so much by God, you "want to know Christ" (Phil. 3:10). You want to spend time daily with Jesus—talking to him and letting him speak to you. You want to spend time in the community of love he has created, with other apprentices of King Jesus. And when you do, something "supernatural" begins to occur. Paul describes it as the energy (*dunamis*, or "dynamite") of King Jesus working powerfully within him. When you choose to open your life up to God, be ready for him to show up in powerful ways. This is King Jesus "dwelling within" you; this is King Jesus "in you," the hope of glory. This is what Paul will refer to later in 3:7 as continuing to "walk" daily with Jesus, "rooted and built up in him," and "rooted and built up in love" (Eph. 3:17). This is the risen Jesus dwelling within our hearts, which is the same as the Holy Spirit, or the Spirit of God's Son, making his home in our hearts.

Maturing in our love with Jesus is our goal as human beings because that is the way we become the humans God created us to be in the first place. Tomorrow, we will think more about how we may mature in King Jesus as Paul continues this theme.

†

Lord Jesus, mature me to be more responsible and caring in all my relationships. Mature me to be able to think more clearly about my life and the world around me by immersing myself in your Word. Help me to remember that you do not desire perfection, you desire invasion. You desire that I continue to let you invade my heart and life. Thank you that when I fail, you call me back to you and mature me by teaching me from my mistakes. I hold on tightly to you so that I may attain the maturity for which you have taken hold so tightly of me.

WALKING HABIT: REMEMBER—YOU'RE ONLY HUMAN

To be human means we are *finite*; we are *limited* creatures. That is how God created us—limited and dependent on him. We run into trouble when we forget that (i.e., the "Fall" in Genesis 3). So, take a load off—don't think it is all up to you because it's not! You can't do it all, and God doesn't expect you to. Instead, he wants you to completely rely upon him. Our limitations are a gift from God that invite us to depend on our Creator. As we depend on him, we come to know, enjoy, and trust him in the process. Jesus' invitation is, "Come to me, if you are weary and burdened, and I will give you rest. Take my yoke upon you (i.e., "hitch up with me and let's do it together") and learn from me, for I am gentle and humble in heart, and you will find rest for our souls" (Matt. 11:28-30). Remind yourself when the pressures mount: "I'm only human, and that is how God designed me. Jesus, I'm turning my anxiety over to you. Bring order to this day and let me rest in you."[4]

---

[4]An excellent book on our limitations being a gift from God is Kelly M. Kapic, *You're Only Human: How Your Limits Reflect God's Design and Why That's Good News* (Ada, MI: Brazos Press, 2022).

WAYS TO MATURE IN KING JESUS

I want you to know how hard I am contending for you and for those at Laodicea, and for all who have not met me personally. 2 My goal is that they may be encouraged in heart and united in love [being knit together in love], so that they may have the full riches of complete understanding in order that they may know the mystery of God, namely, King Jesus [to reach all the riches of full assurance of understanding and the knowledge of God's mystery, which is King Jesus], in whom are hidden all the treasures of wisdom and knowledge. (2:1-3)

Paul has already stated his goal in ministry: to help everyone become mature in their relationship with King Jesus. Although this meant discomfort and prison for Paul, Jesus filled him with Spirit-filled energy (*dunamis*). In these verses, he continues his thought, explaining how hard he is "contending" (*agone*, a word taken from athletic competition) for the Colossians and the neighboring Laodiceans. He describes more ways that we may mature, to become the humans God created us to be according to the blueprint of King Jesus:

1. *We mature in King Jesus as a result of being in a close-knit community of love.*

Paul says his ministry is all about getting people to be "encouraged/comforted" in heart and "knit together" in love in the close-knit community of King Jesus. By being connected with people in Jesus' church, we can grow even deeper in our understanding and experience of God. The church is not an option for believers (or for humans for that matter). The church is actually part of the gospel (Good News) message: "Paul's understanding of community is nothing less than the gospel itself in corporate form!"[1] Paul is not talking about just going to a building on Sunday morning, although corporate worship is a vital part, and Sunday worship is often the place people begin connecting with other Christians. But Paul is going further: our maturity in King Jesus and our deeper experiences of God happen in deeper, close-knit relationships, which is what all humans want (because God made us that way). Paul uses a few phrases to describe what he is talking about:

- *Encouraged/comforted in heart*. The word for "encouraged" here comes from the same root word Jesus uses in John 14-17 to describe the Holy Spirit: *paraklythosin.* Jesus calls the Holy Spirit our "Paraklete," or one who encourages/comforts, literally one who "walks along beside us." Part of how God continues to encourage/comfort/walk beside us is through others. We can't live alone, and we were not created to live alone. Our relationships need to be much deeper than surface level, social media "friends." We need someone who will comfort our hearts. The "God of all comfort (*paraklytos*) comforts us in all our troubles" through other Christians who have the love of God poured into their hearts, so that we may in turn comfort (encour-

---

[1]Robert Banks, *Paul's Idea of Community: The Early House Churches in Their Historical Setting* (Grand Rapids, MI: Eerdmans, 1980), 189.

age) those in trouble with the comfort we receive from God (2 Cor. 1:3,4).

- *Knit together in love.* Paul is talking about allowing ourselves to get deeper in relationship with others, deeper in community. He uses a strong word to describe it: "knit together." Paul uses this term again in 2:19 to describe how we are knit together, just like a body is knit together by ligaments and sinews. How does this deep level of close-knit community happen? Through love. It begins from the love of God; God's love is our Source and our constant fuel and energy. As Christians, we can then come together without any pretenses or fear—everyone is completely accepted, no matter our past, economic status, ethnicity, gender, fears, failures--no matter what. All are accepted at the foot of the cross, and the greatest among us is the one who serves best. And God himself has taught us how to love. The word Paul uses here for love (*agape*) is not feelings or "likes." We are weary of the way the word "loves" or "likes" us; we need people who are committed to us, just like God is forever committed to us. Paul uses the word *agape* (unconditional love) throughout Colossians and his other letters. McKnight says this type of love "describes a person's rugged commitment to another person in three ways: in presence, in advocacy, and in the mutual direction of development toward Christlikeness. Paul, in other words, is not yearning that these folks will simply have affection for one another, but that they will commit themselves to one another as they all grow in Christ into unity."[2]

2. *We mature in King Jesus as we grow deeper in our knowledge and experience of Jesus.* Jesus reveals himself when

[2]McKnight, 209.

"two or three are gathered together in my name" (Matt. 18:20). Being in a close-knit community is not only good for our emotions and souls; it also helps us learn more about just who this God is. "Living in a loving and forgiving community will assist in growth and understanding, and vice versa, as truth is confirmed in practice and practice enables truth to be seen in action and so to be fully grasped."[3] But this happens when we, as a church, keep our focus on *Jesus.* Every sermon, church class, church podcast, church program, church retreat, anything we do together needs to have its center, focus, and grounding on Jesus. Paul stresses this by saying that in Jesus we have all the "riches" of "full assurance," "understanding," and "full knowledge." Paul then underscores this by repeating it is only in Jesus that we know and experience the "mystery of God," which is King Jesus himself, "in whom are hidden all the riches of wisdom and knowledge." Jesus is how we not only come to know what God is like, but our relationship with Jesus takes us deeper into the depths of love and experience of God. There is no "generic God;" the God who created the universe and you and me is none other than the God who reveals himself completely for us in Jesus of Nazareth. "Everything we might want to ask about God and his purposes can and must now be answered with reference to the crucified and risen Jesus, the Messiah."[4]

As we will see later in Colossians 2, there were some saying that people could have "deeper" experiences of God through ecstatic worship and strict disciplinary habits. Paul is eager that we have "deeper" experiences of God, but those are not the ways. Deeper experiences of

---

[3]Wright, *Colossians,* 98.
[4]Wright, *Colossians*, 99.

God come by knowing Jesus more deeply. As Thompson notes, "…knowledge of God and Christ are inseparable and, more, that since the identity of God has been revealed through and in Christ, in order to understand who God is, one must acknowledge God in Christ. All the treasures of wisdom and knowledge are hidden in Christ because all the fullness of God was pleased to dwell in him."[5]

†

Father God and Lord Jesus, thank you that you know my deepest needs. Thank you for fulfilling my deepest needs. Thank you for wishing that I be filled with joy and that my joy might be complete. Thank you that part of my need and source of joy is other people because you made me to be in ever-deepening relationships with others. Help me today to appreciate the people around me. Give me the courage to step out and begin other relationships and deepen existing ones. Thank you, Lord Jesus, for your grace, thank you, Father, for your love, thank you, Spirit, for your fellowship.

WALKING HABIT: TAKE THE NEXT STEP TO DEEPER RELATIONSHIPS

God created us as "communal" humans; we need people to live joy-filled, full lives. But opening ourselves up to others takes courage. Ask God for the courage to deepen your relationships. You can be assured he will give you the courage and that he will begin placing people in your life. If you are not already involved in a church, ask God for the courage to step out in

[5]Thompson, 49, 50.

faith and find a church. If you want to get more connected in a church, ask how you can *serve because one of the best ways to get connected is to get involved in ways to serve others.*

MORE WAYS TO MATURE IN KING JESUS

So then, just as you received Christ Jesus as Lord, continue to live your lives [walk] in him, 7 rooted and built up in him, strengthened in the faith as you were taught, and overflowing with thankfulness. (2:6,7)

...so that you may live a life [walk] worthy of the Lord and please him in every way: bearing fruit in every good work, growing in the knowledge of God, 11 being strengthened with all power according to his glorious might so that you may have great endurance and patience, 12 and giving joyful thanks to the Father. (1:10-12)

I pray that out of his glorious riches he may strengthen you with power through his Spirit in your inner being, 17 so that Christ may dwell in your hearts through faith. And I pray that you, being rooted and established in love, 18 may have power, together with all the Lord's holy people, to grasp how wide and long and high and deep is the love of Christ, 19 and to know this love that surpasses knowledge—that you may be filled to the measure of all the fullness of God. (Eph. 3:16-19)

Our two verses from Colossians today "sum up neatly the message of the entire letter."[1] Paul's goal in ministry and in this letter is that his readers may mature in their relationship with Jesus and consequently mature as human beings. This maturity will always involve being on guard against philosophies that are destructive to us as humans, and these verses are the opening to the rest of Colossians 2, in which Paul addresses head on the destructive philosophy the Colossians are encountering. But the best way to think about any philosophy or worldview we face, the best way to mature in Christ and mature as human beings, is what Paul lays out beautifully in these two verses.

I have included above two parallel passages in which Paul says much the same things in different ways: from Col. 1:10-12 and Eph. 3:16-19. Paul begins from the time we became Christians and then multiplies metaphors to describe how we may experience an ever-deepening, experiential knowledge and relationship with King Jesus:

1. *King Jesus must be LORD*. Paul begins by saying, "just as you received King Jesus as Lord," and he is probably referring to our baptism into Jesus (to which he will refer again in verse 12). As we have noted, Paul's use of the term "Lord" (*kyrios*) is the same word used in the Greek translation of the Old Testament to refer to YHWH, the Creator God of Israel. This is the audacious claim that the Creator God of the universe, the personal God of Israel, has taken on flesh and bone to dwell with us; he has shown up in person to rescue us. But to say "Jesus is Lord" also makes a statement about us and about whom we trust with our lives and how we live. To say, "Jesus is Lord" means we are saying "Jesus is in charge of all of my life." I can trust him because of his great love for me (which love I experience on a deeper

[1]Wright, *Colossians,* 102.

level each day). Because of his great love, I am going to live the way he wants me to live because he absolutely knows best how humans should live, and I know he always has my best interests at heart. But our maturity as humans and in Christ can't proceed unless we truly make Jesus Lord. Jesus said it is impossible to serve two masters (Matt. 6:24). Our previous masters (ourselves, our passions and addictions, our false ways of thinking) were horrible masters and imprisoned us. Jesus is a great Master, and we ironically become freer under his Lordship. As Paul said in Romans 6:

> *You can readily recall, can't you, how at one time the more you did just what you felt like doing—not caring about others, not caring about God—the worse your life became and the less freedom you had? And how much different is it now as you live in God's freedom, your lives healed and expansive in holiness? As long as you did what you felt like doing, ignoring God, you didn't have to bother with right thinking or right living, or right anything for that matter. But do you call that a free life? What did you get out of it? Nothing you're proud of now. Where did it get you? A dead end. But now that you've found you don't have to listen to sin to tell you what to do, and have discovered the delight of listening to God telling you, what a surprise! A whole, healed, put-together life right now, with more and more of life on the way! (Rom. 6:19-22, The Message)*

2. *Walk daily in Him*. Paul shifts from the past tense to the present tense and uses the metaphor of "walking" (*peripateo*), which the NIV translates "live." The word *walking* brings out the force of what Paul is saying. The Jesus relationship needs to be an everyday thing that becomes part of our daily routines, reshaping our daily habits. Our habits and

our friends make us the people we will turn out to be, and Jesus must reshape both. The Psalmist used the metaphor of walking in Psalm 1 to describe the person who is "happy" and blessed in life: they "walk not" with people or friends that are not good for them, but instead their delight is in the Word (the Torah) of God, and they saturate themselves daily with the Word, like a tree planted by streams of water. In the process, their lives become flourishing and fruitful. Paul repeatedly uses the term "walking" in the present tense, emphasizing that our "walk with the Lord" must be an ongoing, daily routine (see 1 Thess. 2:12, 4:12; Col. 1:10; Eph. 4:1, 5:8; Rom. 6:4).

3. *Be "rooted" in the love of King Jesus*. Paul next uses the metaphor of a plant growing, much as he did in Col. 1:10 about Jesus "bearing fruit" in our lives. Here he says, "be rooted" in Jesus, which is a beautiful metaphor of how the in-dwelling Jesus grows in our lives. King Jesus has to take root, deep down. Jesus used similar metaphors throughout his teaching, particularly in the parable of the sower (Mark 4:1-20; Matt. 13:1-23). In this parable, the abundance of the crops didn't depend on the seed, it depended on how *receptive* the soil was and whether there were other things in the soil interfering and impeding the growth. The point here is that King Jesus needs to get down deep into our souls, down into all the deep secrets and desires of our hearts. The Root needs to take hold deep down. I love the parallel passage in Eph. 3:16-17 because there Paul uses another term to describe what we are "rooted" in: the Love of King Jesus. Being rooted in King Jesus means first and foremost being "rooted" in his unbelievable, "never-giving up on us" kind of love.

As humans, we live by our loves. Our habits and our actions always reveal who or what we "love" at our deepest level. And that is how we change, how we can mature as human beings: *we have to change our loves*. Jesus is waiting and eager to start a love relationship with you and change your deep down loves. Spend daily time walking with him to let your roots go down deep into his love.

4. *Be strengthened [constantly confirmed] in the faithfulness you were taught*. Paul next uses a metaphor from law, with the idea that our relationship with Jesus becomes validated or confirmed, just as a lawyer's argument might be confirmed by evidence. So, what validates or confirms our relationship with Jesus, what "evidence" convinces us that he should be Lord of our lives? Paul says, "in the faith as you were taught." Faith can also mean "faithfulness," and the force of what Paul is saying is that our relationship with Jesus is *validated by his faithfulness to us*. Paul says we should let Jesus validate his faithfulness "as you were taught," reminding us that we need to be *daily* "renewing our minds" with the Word of God, letting the "word of Christ" dwell in us richly.

5. *Be overflowing with thanksgiving*. Becoming thankful people is never far from Paul's mind as he stresses in this letter how important it is for us as Christians and as human beings to learn to be thankful on a daily basis (see 1:3, 1:12, 2:7, 3:15, 16,17, 4:2). A funny thing about thanksgiving: it feeds on itself. The more we remember to be thankful, the more thankful we become, and the more things we realize we have to be thankful for. Pretty soon thankfulness is "overflowing." Learning to become thankful is also a daily thing—we need to "walk in thankfulness." Try it today. Begin starting every day and ending every day thinking of

things you have to be thankful for, and your list will grow every day. The greatest thing to be thankful for is the deep, selfless, constant, never to be doubted, faithful love of God that is in King Jesus our Lord.

†

King Jesus, I praise you that you are the Great Master. Today, I make you Lord. I give up those things in my life that I have either made or have let become my "masters." I know you have the power to break the strongholds in my life, and I surrender them completely to you right now. I know that their hold on me can only be demolished by your more powerful love. I give all my affection completely to you. Fill me with your love and transform my loves. I commit to spending time daily with you to let your love pour into my heart, to listen to your Word and let it clear my mind and bring me peace. I praise you for having set my heart and mind free!

WORSHIP HABIT: REMEMBER TO SAY "THANKS!"

Begin and end each day thinking about the good things in your life and say, "Thank you, God." Each week, write down at least 10 things that you are grateful for (maybe even start a Gratitude Journal). When someone does something for you, make sure you say "Thanks." Giving thanks changes your whole attitude about life. Instead of letting your mind dwell on things that bring fear or sadness, remember to give thanks in every situation.

THE HOLLOW AND DECEPTIVE PHILOSOPHIES IN PAUL'S DAY

> *I tell you this so that no one may deceive you by fine-*
> *sounding arguments. 5 For though I am absent from*
> *you in body, I am present with you in spirit and delight*
> *to see how disciplined you are and how firm your faith*
> *in Christ is....See to it that no one takes you captive*
> *through hollow and deceptive philosophy, which de-*
> *pends on human tradition and the elemental spiritual*
> *forces of this world rather than on Christ. 9 For in*
> *Christ all the fullness of the Deity lives in bodily*
> *form, 10 and in Christ you have been brought to full-*
> *ness. He is the head over every power and authority.*
> *(2:4-5, 8-10)*

Thus far in their letter, Paul and Timothy have been circling around this philosophy that is invading the young Colossian church, and now they address it head on. They have mentioned how important are "wisdom," "knowledge," and "understanding," and have stressed that God himself has given us "full knowledge," true wisdom, and correct understanding about our world through King Jesus. But not everyone believes in King Jesus, and there were a lot of different philosophies contending for people's minds in Paul's and Timothy's day, just as there are today. Paul is not opposed to philosophy, which literally means "love of wisdom." What Paul wants us to see is that any philosophy that is not rooted in the love of God and that does not acknowledge God's authority (as our Creator) to tell us the truth is "deceptive" and "hollow." Such philosophies actually "rob us" and "take us captive." Paul and Timothy want us to be aware and alert. *We Christians need to think deeply about the times in which we live!*

Colossians 2:6 through 3:4 is one long, connected passage, and it would be helpful to read it all in one setting. Paul weaves and connects a lot of different thoughts and arguments. Although what Paul and Timothy were confronting in Colossians is different from the various philosophies we confront today, there are parallels. Today, let's look at what Paul and Timothy were confronting in their day, and tomorrow we will look at some parallel "philosophies" we are facing in our world today.

Empty Philosophies Then

The details of the philosophy Paul and Timothy were confronting are found in 2:16-23. Here in a nutshell are some of those details and how Paul and Timothy address them:

- Paul tells us in 2:8 not to be taken captive by hollow and deceptive human philosophies based on human perceptions and emotions rather than on King Jesus, who created humans. Paul calls these philosophies "elemental spiritual forces of this world" (*stoichea tou kosmos*). Originally, *stoichea* meant the basic chemical elements of the world (earth, air, water, and fire), but it came to be used to describe local deities whose power influenced the world. Paul is saying that human philosophies have tremendous power to influence people. Whether or not we realize it, the ideas and prevailing worldviews of our culture affect us and our families every day. Like the air we breathe, they are all around us and influence us without us even realizing it. Paul counters all philosophies by saying that in King Jesus, God has given us all his "fullness" in a human, understandable, truth-revealing way. All the truths about us as humans and everything we need to live flourishing lives are found in King Jesus, in his Spirit and Word that actively works in our hearts and minds, and in his body, the church community.

- The particular philosophy that Paul and Timothy were addressing was a form of Jewish philosophy that promised its adherents both acceptance by God and heightened spiritual awareness (which could lead to ecstatic spiritual experiences such as worshipping with angels). The path for both acceptance by God and heightened spirituality was for one to convert to Judaism and adopt Jewish practices (which Paul calls "works of the Law" in Galatians and Romans). These included observing Jewish ceremonial rules (what to eat and drink, and observing strict Jewish Sabbath regulations and Jewish festivals). For males, this particularly meant circumcision, which for Jews was the crucial entry point into the true people of God. In Galatians 4:3, Paul again calls these "works of the Law" (Jewish ceremonial rules) "elemental spiritual forces of this world" (*stoichea tou kosmos*). What Paul meant by the term "works of the Law" (both in Colossians and in Galatians) was not some form of legalism. Rather, it was a form of *Jewish nationalism*. As Wright says, "Paul's critique of Judaism does not aim, as in the old caricature, at 'legalism,' the supposed attempt to earn righteousness through good works. It aims at the position of national superiority which Judaism had thought to claim on the basis of God's choice of her."[1] As

[1]Wright, *Colossians,* 33.

Paul argues in Galatians, the Jewish ceremonial practices were a "custodian" until the time had fully come for Jesus to be born into this world. Jesus is the fulfillment of the Law that renders obsolete the Jewish ceremonial practices. All are now accepted by God when they put their faith in Jesus, so that "there is neither Jew nor Gentile, slave nor free, male nor female, for you are all one in Christ Jesus" (Gal. 3:23-29).

- The philosophy also taught that a person needed to live a very strict, disciplined, and rule-based life. Paul calls it "harsh treatment of the body," and even quotes its mantra: "Do not handle! Do not taste! Do not touch!" This is one form of *dualism*, the belief that the body and the soul/mind are separate from each other. Dualism was prevalent in Greek philosophy. The Colossian philosophers were promoting a dualism that the mind must subject the body to extreme harshness to keep it in line and attain true spiritual awareness. Another form of dualism that Christians encountered in the first century was known as "Gnosticism," a philosophy that claimed "secret and hidden wisdom for the elite," but believed that spirit alone was good, and the body was evil. It didn't matter what you did with your body; your mind and inner self was your true self (which sounds very similar to philosophies of today). Thus, the Gnostics would engage in all kinds of sexual immorality and claim they could still attain Divine knowledge and wisdom in their mind and spirit.[2] Paul and the early Christians countered dualism with the understanding that humans are both body and soul/mind, that everything God

[2]Paul confronts this type of Gnostic dualism in the Corinthian church (see, e.g., 1 Cor. 6:12-20), and John confronts this type of Gnostic dualism in 1 John (see, e.g., 1 John 3:4-10).

made was good, including the body, and that humans should honor God with their bodies (see 1 Tim. 4:4; 1 Cor. 6:12-20).

- Paul counters that we, as Christians, should not let the world "judge us" by its human standards. King Jesus, as the Creator of the universe, is the source of all philosophies and powers. Although philosophy in itself is a good thing (because all truth is God's truth), any way of viewing life that loses connection with King Jesus becomes distorted and destructive. Humans have a tendency to take some good thing (such as care for the marginalized) and twist it as a means to gain power or for other selfish purposes. A good example are current movements that call for "social justice" but seek this justice in very unjust and unloving ways.
- King Jesus won't let the world "judge" us by its distorted standards. The truth about us and about all of life is found in his powerful, gracious truth. King Jesus offers forgiveness and freedom to everyone, including those who are trapped in the deceptions of empty philosophies. King Jesus has disarmed all the powers and pervading cultural trends of this age and every age, and he has done so by stooping to rescue us, taking upon himself all the accusations the world can hurl at us.

These were the philosophies Paul and Timothy were combating in the first century. Tomorrow, we will explore parallels of these philosophies that we encounter in our day. But in every age, people have been able to break free from human philosophies that dehumanize us by listening to the Voice of the One Who speaks the Truth, King Jesus.

†

King Jesus, I praise you that you speak truth about our world and about humanity. Help me today to think about our current world and culture through your eyes and through the lens of your truth. King Jesus, you have outlasted every human philosophy, and you will outlast all the philosophies in our world today. You make sense of history and humanity, and I praise you for your gracious and truthful presence in my life.

HOLLOW AND DECEPTIVE PHILOSOPHIES TODAY (PART 1)

My goal is that they may be encouraged in heart and united in love, so that they may have the full riches of complete understanding, in order that they may know the mystery of God, namely, Christ, 3 in whom are hidden all the treasures of wisdom and knowledge. 4 I tell you this so that no one may deceive you by fine-sounding arguments.... See to it that no one takes you captive through hollow and deceptive philosophy, which depends on human tradition and the elemental spiritual forces of this world rather than on Christ. 9 For in Christ all the fullness of the Deity lives in bodily form, 10 and in Christ you have been brought to fullness. He is the head over every power and authority. (2:2-4, 8-10)

Colossians is a "worldview" book. As John Barclay writes, Colossians provides "an integrated view of reality" and "a comprehensive vision of truth—cosmic and human, spiritual and material, divine and mundane—whose focal point is [Christ]."[1] As Walsh and Keesmaat note, Colossians

[1]John Barclay, *Colossians*, 77.

> …tells us who rules the world, where the world has come from and where it is going, where wisdom is ultimately to be found, and even which community of people holds the promise and destiny of the world in its hearts and lives.[2]

Paul's and Timothy's words still speak to us today because our world is full of competing voices, shouting at us to abide by their ways of thinking. The world of the first century was hostile to the Christian message, and our world is similarly hostile and becoming more so each day. Below are some prevailing philosophies of our day that have parallels in the letter to the Colossians. As Paul and Timothy said, we need to make sure we are not "taken captive" to these hollow and deceptive philosophies, that we don't let the world "judge us," and that we stay closely connected to King Jesus, his message, and his community. Today we will think about how little value our culture places on the human body in contrast to the way we were created. Tomorrow, we will think about the pervading philosophies of tribalism/nationalism and Eastern mysticism.

Dualism. Just as Greek and Gnostic dualism pervaded the first century, a dualism that separates the body from "personhood" permeates our culture. As Nancy Pearcey masterfully describes in *Love Thy Body: Answering Hard Questions about Life and Sexuality*, our culture has adopted a "two-story" view of life and humanity.[3] In this two-story world, values and morals are "subjective and personal," while science and facts are objective and "real." Similarly, the body is seen as unimportant or not relevant to our humanity. This worldview gets played out in the following hot button issues:

---

[2]Walsh and Keesmaat, 99.
[3]Pearcey, 12.

- *Abortion.* Proponents of abortion (and the Supreme Court decisions on abortion) rest on the presumption that although an embryo has life, it is not a "person." The baby in the womb is not yet a person because (as far as we know!) it has not yet achieved a certain level of consciousness. Such dualism is scary because it puts us all in peril. As Pearcey notes, this personhood theory "presumes a very low view of the human body, which ultimately dehumanizes all of us. For if our bodies do not have inherent value, then a key part of our identity is devalued. What we discover is that this same body/person dichotomy, with its denigration of the body, is the unspoken assumption driving secular values on euthanasia, sexuality, homosexuality, transgenderism, and a host of related ethical issues."[4]
- *Sexuality.* Our sexualized culture emphasizes in so many ways that sex is just something we do with our bodies that has no effect on our soul and spirit. "This is sex cut off from the whole person—sex as an exchange of physical services between autonomous, disconnected individuals."[5] But because humans are *embodied* people, sexual encounters deeply affect our emotions and spirits. Our culture of casual sex is creating a wasteland where people don't know how to have lasting, committed relationships, and where people become sadly addicted to pornography. Sex is a beautiful, intimate, bonding gift that God gives us. In a sexual encounter, hormones such as oxytocin are released. Oxytocin creates a strong emotional feeling of trust, or as one therapist said, it "creates an involuntary chemical

---

[4]Pearcey, 20.
[5]Pearcey, 28.

commitment."[6] Although we may think sex is casual, our bodies don't lie to us. As Lauren Winner translates Paul's words from 1 Cor. 6:16: "Don't you know that when you sleep with someone, your body makes a promise, whether you do or not?"[7] But God wants to make us whole, to heal our emotions by bringing body and soul back together in the way he created us. "Biblical morality asks us to be consistent with what we say with our bodies and what we say with the rest of our lives. To tell the truth with our bodies."[8]

- *Transgenderism*. Dualism has reached its logical conclusion in the transgender movement.[9] "Today, the accepted treatment is not to help people change their inner feelings of gender identity to match their body, but to change their body (through hormones and surgery) to match their feelings. In other words, when a person senses a dissonance between body and mind, the mind wins. The body is dismissed as irrelevant."[10] Unfortunately, the sudden rise of the transgender movement has created what psychologists call "Rapid-Onset Gender Dysphoria" among teens and young adults: people who had no prior signs of gender dysphoria suddenly becoming trans because it is popular in our culture and on social media.[11] Studies are showing that

[6]Theresa Crenshaw, *The Alchemy of Love and Lust*, cited in Jennifer Roback Morse, *Sexual Revolution and its Victims: Thirty-Five Prophetic Articles Spanning Two Decades* (Lake Charles, La: The Ruth Institute, 2015), 150.
[7]Lauren Winner, *Real Sex* (Grand Rapids: Brazos Press, 2006), 88.
[8]Pearcey, 137.
[9]There is now much good literature addressing the transgender movement from a Christian perspective, and one of the best is Preston Sprinkle's *Embodied: Transgender Identities, the Church, and What the Bible Has to Say* (Colorado Springs, CO: David C. Cook, 2021).
[10]Pearcey, 194-195.
[11]Sprinkle, *Embodied*, 159-177.

many who have transitioned through hormones or surgery later deeply regret it, as evidenced by the "Detransition Advocacy Network."[12] Christians need to speak the truth about humanity into these discussions, but we need to speak it in love. Our culture has messed people up, and only the grace and truth of Jesus can heal them. As Preston Sprinkle writes, "We need less outrage and more outrageous love. What we need is a different way. A radically biblical community. One that affirms bodies, rejects stereotypes, pursues truth with humility, and lavishes grace on everyone who fails."[13]

†

Creator God, our loving Abba Father and King Jesus, thank you for creating such a beautiful and exquisite world. Thank you for my body and for creating me as an embodied soul. Thank you for creating such harmony in nature by ordering things according to your love and goodness. I am thankful that you bring order to my body and soul. King Jesus, help me to notice and pray for a hurting world, and show me today how I can be involved in bringing your reconciliation to a world desperate for grace and truth. I love you.

---

[12]Sprinkle, 173.
[13]Sprinkle, 224.

HOLLOW AND DECEPTIVE PHILOSOPHIES TODAY (PART 2)

My goal is that they may be encouraged in heart and united in love so that they may have the full riches of complete understanding, in order that they may know the mystery of God, namely, Christ, 3 in whom are hidden all the treasures of wisdom and knowledge. 4 I tell you this so that no one may deceive you by fine-sounding arguments.... See to it that no one takes you captive through hollow and deceptive philosophy, which depends on human tradition and the elemental spiritual forces of this world rather than on Christ. 9 For in Christ all the fullness of the Deity lives in bodily form, 10 and in Christ you have been brought to fullness. He is the head over every power and authority. (2:2-4, 8-10)

Previously, we looked at the dualism that pervades our secular culture. Today, we will look at two other dominant philosophies: tribalism/nationalism and Eastern mysticism.

Tribalism and Nationalism. The lack of shared values in the United States has created what sociologists call "identity politics:" groups with shared beliefs and values resorting to politics to gain as much political power as possible. If there is no right and wrong, then morality becomes a matter of power and control, and thus politics is given paramount importance. The result, however, is tribalism where people talk past each other, compromise is unacceptable, and government goes from bad to worse (which is our current political climate). Because of the chaos created by our current secular culture, Christians sometimes put more faith in politics than in Jesus Christ working through his Spirit, Word and his church. This has given rise to *Christian nationalism*, which is dangerous, idolatrous, and damages the truth of the Good News of Jesus Christ.

Christian nationalism is more than love of country or seeking to preserve the Christian principles on which our nation was founded. Christian nationalists don't just believe that America was founded on Christian principles; they believe America is and should always be a Christian nation.[1] The following are some of the problems with Christian nationalism:

- *Christian nationalism is unrealistic and impossible in our multicultural, pluralistic society*. America is made up of many different cultures and ethnic backgrounds. Trying to impose a nostalgic, Protestant Christian heritage on this rich cultural landscape is not only impossible, it impedes the vitality of the Christian gospel, which encompasses people from all tribes, languages and nations.
- *Christian nationalism becomes undemocratic and illiberal.* Instead of recognizing the dignity, freedom, and worth of every human being, it tries to coerce others to accept a Christian heritage. It relies on force instead of persuasion, legislation instead of the Spirit of God working in the hearts and minds of people.

---

[1]Paul D. Miller, *The Religion of American Greatness: What's Wrong with Christian Nationalism* (Downers Grove, Il: InterVarsity Press, 2022), 39.

- *Christian nationalism backfires and causes more division among Americans than unity.* "Much of American evangelicalism is acting more like a cultural tribe, an ethnoreligious sect advocating for its own power and protection, rather than a people from every tribe and nation advocating for universal principles of justice, flourishing, and the common good."[2]
- *Christian nationalism can become idolatrous, and when it does, Jesus will be used by politicians for personal gain, not for the purposes of Jesus.* While love of country is good, if it is not submitted to the Lordship of Jesus, it can become a god in itself, and this is especially so when power becomes more important than principal. As C. S. Lewis said, love of country can become "a demon when it becomes a god."[3] When Christians become too aligned with any one political party, there is a grave danger in becoming just another tool to be used by politicians. Politicians have always recognized the power of religion and have tried to use it to further their own political purposes. Christians should be suspicious and critical of politics and should not hesitate to renounce politicians who lie, belittle, or cause unnecessary divisions. The church should be the "conscience of the state," not the lackey of any politician.

Mysticism. Christianity has had a long, beautiful history of mysticism.[4] Jesus' profound description of his desire that the love of Father God and King Jesus be in us, and that Jesus himself be "in us," can only be described as *mystical*. So too could

---

[2]Miller, 7.

[3]C.S. Lewis, *The Four Loves* (New York: Hartcourt and Brace, 1960), 39.

[4]See, for example, *Light from Light: An Anthology of Christian Mysticism*, Louis Dupre and James A. Wieseman, eds. (Mahwah, NJ: Paulist Press, 1988).

Paul's prayer in Ephesians 3 (and elsewhere) that we be "filled to the full measure of all the fullness of God" (Eph. 3:19). As Christians, we should in a very real sense be "Jesus mystics" through deep, contemplative prayer, solitude, and meditation on Scripture. But there is a mysticism that is dangerous to us as humans because it is pursued either for purely selfish reasons (as was the Colossian heresy) or as an escape from reality instead of the connection with Reality. This is Eastern mysticism, which is so prevalent in our culture. Eastern mysticism teaches that good and evil co-exist eternally—the yin and the yang. The goal of Eastern mysticism is nirvana, the escape from this cycle of good and evil. As Dr. Timothy Jennings notes, this escape does not deal with our actual selfishness and fear, nor does this type of mysticism desire to change our selfishness and fear. "Eastern practices create an illusion in which one feels as if they are healed and transformed into a nondual, unified, healthy state, when in actuality they remain infected with fear and selfishness."[5] Christian prayer and meditation, on the other hand, connects our spirits to the very Spirit of God, who transforms us to become whole, fearless, and selfless, reflecting his character.

As Christians, we need to meditate. Not a meditation that escapes reality, but rather a meditation that connects to Reality. As Jesus said, we need to "go into your room, close the door, and pray to Abba Father, and Abba Father, who sees what is done in secret, will reward you" (Matt. 6:6). We connect with the Reality that is the love of God, the love that loved us first and that has shown the full extent of that love in Jesus. As Henri Nouwen said, to be "safely anchored in the knowledge of

---

[5]Jennings, *The God Shaped Brain*, 224.

God's first love, we have to be mystics. A mystic is a person whose identity is deeply rooted in God's first love."[6]

†

Lord Jesus, you are the true King, and you have changed everything we think about power. Forgive us when, out of fear, we love power instead of letting you fill us with the power of your love. We don't trust in chariots; we trust in the character of the Lord our God. Give me your wisdom, Jesus, in thinking about the issues in our world today. I pray for our nation and for all the nations in this world that we may come to know you through Jesus our King, and that we may become a kingdom of priests to rule wisely in truth, justice, and mercy. I hold up your name, King Jesus, and praise you!

WALKING HABIT: ENCOUNTER GOD IN PRAYER

As Tim Keller writes, "Prayer is a conversation that leads to an encounter with God."[7] The practice of prayer begins as we meditate on the goodness and love of God, and then feel His invitation to go deeper in communion with Him. It is letting God connect what your mind knows about God to your emotions. God, whom you know with your mind is love, tells you personally, "I love you and will take care of you. You can trust me." As Jonathan Edwards wrote, it is the difference in knowing that honey is sweet and tasting honey. "Taste and see that

[6]Henri J.M. Nouwen, *In the Name of Jesus: Reflections on Christian Leadership* (New York: Crossroad Book, 1989), 42.
[7]Keller, *Prayer,* 165.

the LORD is good" (Ps. 34:8). This encounter and intimacy take time. We don't rush our other love relationships, and intimacy with God will also not grow without allowing "leisurely" time in intimacy with the Father, King Jesus, and the Spirit of truth and love. Prepare your mind for prayer by meditating on Scripture. Don't rush prayer—give time for your mind to rest and become still. Ask God to come into your mind and emotions. As you contemplate the Almighty, you might speak the Lord's prayer, turning every phrase over to God. A great resource that might help you in the practice of prayer is Tim Keller's *Prayer: Experiencing the Awe and Intimacy of God.*

GOD FILLED JESUS, JESUS FILLS US

> *For in Christ all the fullness of the Deity lives [dwells] in bodily form, and in Christ you have been brought to fullness. He is the head over every power and authority. (2:9, 10)*

> *And I pray that you, being rooted and established in love, may have power, together with all the Lord's holy people, to grasp how wide and long and high and deep is the love of Christ, and to know this love that surpasses knowledge—that you may be filled to the measure of all the fullness of God. (Eph. 3:18, 19)*

Paul now tells us why we should not be held "captive" or "robbed" by empty and deceptive philosophies: "for" (because) we have been given "fullness" in King Jesus. Fullness (*plyroma*) is the key word here, and because all the "fullness" of the Godhead dwelt in Jesus, so now that same God-given "fullness" of life can dwell in us. The thief (all the half-truths and empty promises of this world) comes to steal, kill, and destroy; King Jesus comes to give us real, quality life, and life to the full! (John 10:10). We don't have to be held captive any longer to the dead-end ways and philosophies of the world for the following reasons:

1. *In King Jesus, all the fullness of the Godhead dwells in a human body.* God (the incomprehensible Creator of this universe) is a Spirit, but he desires to "dwell" with us, to make himself known and real in our lives. In the Old Testament, he very tangibly journeyed with the people of Israel through the wilderness (in a cloud by day and fireball by night), and then his Spirit filled the tabernacle (and later the temple) with such thickness the priests couldn't even enter (Ex. 40:34, 35; 1 Kings 8:11ff). This dense cloud had a brightness to it such that the face of those entering into the cloud, the very Presence of Almighty God, would be sunburnt and glow. The Jews described this bright "Presence" (Hebrew *Shekinah*) as the "glory" of God (Hebrew *kabod*, meaning "weighty" or "heavy"). But now God has gone even further: all of his Shekinah glory now dwells in a human body, in Jesus, God with us. "This is a breathtaking claim because it implies that in Christ we see God most clearly…the creator and covenant God who became present in Israel's history is now fully present in the embodied (and glorified) life of Jesus."[1]

   The fact that God (the Creator of human bodies) inhabited a human body at one point in time is remarkable. But it is also remarkable that the risen and glorified Jesus (God the Son) is still embodied in a glorified, human body. Paul uses the present tense when he says that all the fullness of God dwells bodily. What this means is "that Christ's taking on a human nature was not a temporary expedient, to be left behind when he finished the work of salvation. Because he was taken bodily into heaven, his human nature is permanently connected to his divine nature."[2] The risen and ascended Je-

[1]McKnight, 229.
[2]Pearcey, 37.

sus is our assurance that we, too, will receive a glorified, indestructible body one day. This should have a profound impact on the way we view our bodies. Our secular culture teaches us in so many ways to believe "I am not my body." As we have seen, this mindset gets played out in issues such as abortion (an infant is not a "person"), sexuality, and transgenderism. This worldview dehumanizes us. In stark and beautiful contrast, "Christianity holds that body and soul together form an integrated unity—that the human being is an embodied soul."[3] Humans are not just minds that can manipulate our bodies in any way we feel. Nor does a person lose their humanity because they are an unborn infant or because they have somehow lost their "usefulness" to society because of age or disability. We are *embodied* people. Our bodies are part of who we are. By embodying himself in a human body, God has dignified our bodies and has restored a necessary wholeness between body and mind.

2. *In King Jesus, we have in turn been given fullness.* God wants to fill us with himself and by that fullness we receive everything that comes from being surrounded and filled with God: unconditional love, peace and rest, joy, purpose, meaning, character, satisfaction and contentment, trusting and enduring relationships, confidence, and "overflowing hope by the power of the Holy Spirit" (Rom. 15:13). As John said, "Out of his fullness we have all received grace upon grace" (Jn. 1:16). By coming into King Jesus and letting him dwell in our hearts, we "participate in the divine nature, having escaped the corruption of the world caused by evil desires" (2 Peter 1:4). What God desires so much (and God humbled himself in love to bring about) is that we might be "filled to the full measure of all the fullness of God" (Eph. 3:19).

[3]Pearcey, 21.

C.S. Lewis phrases this thought so well:

> If you want to get wet, you must get into the water. And if you want joy, power, peace, eternal life, you must get close to or even into the thing that has them. These are not just some sort of prizes which God hands out. They are the great fountain of energy and beauty spurting up at the very center of reality. Once a person is united to God, they come as gifts, and that person could not help but live forever.[4]

†

Creator God, our Abba Father and our Lord Jesus the King, thank you for creating bodies. Lord Jesus, thank you that even now, in heaven, you still bear our humanity in some way, and particularly by your wounds suffered for us. This means you will never, ever give up on humanity. This means our bodies are beautiful and reflect your love and creativity. This means that nature means something, and there is an integrated wholeness between nature and our spirits, and that we should not fight against the grain of the universe you created. I want to be whole and to learn to glorify you with my body. But I am reminded that nature is broken and not the way you created it to be, and that all of creation groans until the sons and daughters of God are revealed. But the glorious, risen body of King Jesus means that my broken body will be ultimately healed by you in a new, glorious earth when you come to dwell with us forever. May you, Creator God and Lord Jesus Christ, be glorified in my body today.

---

[4]C.S. Lewis, *Mere Christianity* (New York: Macmillan, 1943), 153.

THE CIRCUMCISION PERFORMED BY KING JESUS

In him you were also circumcised with a circumcision not performed by human hands. Your whole self ruled by the flesh was put off when you were circumcised by Christ [in the circumcision of Christ], 12 having been buried with him in baptism, in which you were also raised with him through your faith in the working of God, who raised him from the dead. (2:11, 12)

As we have seen, the empty philosophy that was plaguing the Colossian church had many Jewish elements to it. These false teachers were claiming that if someone wanted to have heightened spiritual awareness and mystical experiences, they had to observe Jewish practices such as observing the Old Testament religious festivals, Sabbath (Saturday) observance, and circumcision (see 2:16,17). Circumcision was one of the most important Jewish rituals because circumcision was the entry point of access to God for males and their families. (My apologies for having to repeat the word *circumcision*, but stay with me—it's important to get Paul's message here and circumcision is the object lesson). God had made an eternal covenant of love for humanity through Abraham and his family, and God commanded that Abraham and his male descendants be circumcised as a "sign" of that covenant (Gen. 17:9-14). But for Jesus and the early Christians, the ceremonial practices of the Old Testament all find their fulfillment in Jesus, God dwelling with us (Matt. 5:17; Gal. 3: 23-29). In Col. 2:17, Paul calls all of these Jewish practices a *foreshadowing* of the "reality" found in King Jesus.

God had always told the Jews that mere circumcision in the flesh (as a physical act) was just a sign of what God wanted most: "circumcision of the heart" (see Deut. 10:16; 30:6-7; Lev. 26:40). "Circumcision of the heart" means a person humbly recognizes her deep need for God and his ways. Paul picks up on this in Romans 2:28, when he says, "A person is not a Jew who is one only outwardly, nor is circumcision merely outward and physical. No, a person is a Jew who is one inwardly, and circumcision is circumcision of the heart, by the Spirit, not by the written code."

Both physical circumcision and "circumcision of the heart" now find their complete fulfillment in King Jesus. What Jewish circumcision was intended to convey—a person coming into the faithful, covenant love of God and committing himself to God—is now fully provided by King Jesus for everyone: female as well as male, Gentiles as well as Jews ("There is neither Jew nor Gentile, slave nor free, male nor female, for you are all one in Christ Jesus. If you belong to Christ, then you are Abraham's seed and heirs according to God's promise"—Gal. 3:28). There is no need for a Gentile to be physically circumcised to come into the covenant love of God. God has already performed all that needs to be done for us to come into his covenant of love; he did it in King Jesus, who was stripped and cut up on our behalf. King Jesus himself, with his outstretched, nail-scarred hands, is our entry point into God's love. We are now circumcised with a circumcision performed by God's hands, the "circumcision of Christ." Jesus, the reality of what circumcision foreshadowed, is our access and entry point into the Presence of God and all the fullness he gives us.

Paul makes a connection in this passage between Jewish circumcision (which was the entry point to the covenant love of God) and baptism into Christ (which is the "entry point" when we accept Jesus as our King and Savior). We should not think of baptism as some sort of prerequisite to being accepted by God. Baptism is instead *a gift from God*, something God gives us that powerfully symbolizes, in a very physical way, our entry into the covenant love of God in King Jesus. "Baptism is not what we do, but what God does."[1]

God himself came up with the idea of baptism because it is a beautiful, physical picture of coming into all that God has done for us in Jesus. First of all, we have to surrender and "take the plunge"--our whole selves, body and mind, surrender to the love of God. We give up. We've reached the point that we admit we really don't know what's best for us; we really can't become the people we want to become on our own; we really can't live without the love and purpose God gives. So, we dive into the love of God, leaving all of our past--all that we've done, all that people have done to us, all of our old habits and desires, all of our fears, and every dark power that controls us. We let King Jesus "strip it away." We die to ourselves. But what we are dying *into* is the love of God, and we see that love so fully in the death of King Jesus for us. So we go under the water, which in a beautiful way portrays us burying our old life and being buried into the love of God in the cross. But then, just as King Jesus came back to life, becoming King over death and every other power, we too rise with him. We rise out of the water, cleansed, free, made completely new, with the assured hope that God will never, ever give up on us.

---

[1]McKnight, 239.

King Jesus has committed himself to us forever, and we can always look back on our baptism and say, “that was my wedding day, when I surrendered to the beautiful love of God.” God has entered into a forever covenant with us in Jesus, and we are his covenant partners. We are also now his apprentices, and he is our Master Teacher in how to live life to the full. God has co-raised us with him by the power of his resurrection into his current, vibrant Kingdom—Jesus’ love, rule, power, and protection.

†

Jesus, you are my Lord because you have seized my heart with your love. Out of your passionate love for me, you stooped down and rescued me. You have ravished my heart, and I have come to know that you always have my best interests at heart. Other loves of my life have let me down and even enslaved me, but you set me free and are making me freer every day. I will root my life today in your love, truth, wisdom, and peace.

WALKING HABIT: BE BAPTIZED

If you haven’t yet been baptized into King Jesus, God himself calls you to be baptized. Baptism is a gift God has given you. Like the Lord’s Supper (Communion, the Eucharist), baptism is a very *physical* act created by the God who made creation and us as embodied people. In this physical act, God meets us. We bring our whole bodies, souls, spirits, and minds into the Love of God embodied in Jesus our King, receiving his Spirit into our hearts and souls. Any Christian can baptize you, and if you prefer, you can be baptized in a private ceremony with just a few friends. If you haven't yet been baptized, open yourself to God's gift of baptism.

GOD MADE YOU ALIVE!

> *When you were dead in your sins and in the uncircumcision of your flesh, God made you alive with Christ. He forgave us all our sins, 14 having canceled the charge of our legal indebtedness, which stood against us and condemned us; he has taken it away, nailing it to the cross. 15 And having disarmed the powers and authorities, he made a public spectacle of them, triumphing over them by the cross. (2:13-15)*

When a person comes to King Jesus, a new creation has begun in every way. The old is gone; the new has come (2 Cor. 5:17). The emphasis in this passage is that just as God raised Jesus from the dead and seated him *right now* above all rule and authority, God has also raised us up with King Jesus and seated us *right now* beside him, under King Jesus' protection, power and authority. God has made us alive, beginning now in this world and with the full assurance that even though we die in this world, we will live again in the new creation. *God has made you alive!* How has he done this?

God has "Graced" us with his love. The word for forgiveness here literally means "gracing" us (*chorizomai*) (Paul uses it again in Col. 3:13). God has covered us with his grace and love by forgiving us. Forgiveness is powerful because it is the way we escape the power of the past. We can't undo what we have done or what others have done to us. But we don't have to live in bondage to it; God's forgiveness is the way out. God's forgiveness doesn't mean we "just forget it and move on." It means God gets involved in our all of our hurt and all of our shame. He takes the load off our shoulders and bears it himself. He continues to "grace" us so that even our emotions about our guilt and our bitterness from being hurt can change and heal over time. That is what love does. Grace and forgiveness change the trajectory of our lives. It heals our wounds and turns them into opportunities to help others who are in bondage to the same hurts and destructive habits. Forgiveness is the path to a new future, a new hope, a new you.

King Jesus has taken away the power of guilt and accusation. Paul provides a powerful picture here of how God's grace and forgiveness opens the path to a new future. Paul says King Jesus canceled the "written code against us." This "written code" could be the righteous law of God (the Old Testament Torah). Some scholars see it as an allusion to the Jewish understanding that God kept a great "scorecard" of our lives. Paul recognizes that this "written code" is right about us: we do fail to live up to what we should be as humans. We know our failings deep in our hearts, and it pains us. We can't gloss over our failures; God's law is correct in pointing out our mistakes. But the law can only accuse; it can't save. And that is what King Jesus has done—he has canceled all the accusations that are rightfully directed at us. Paul uses two images to drive this home. First, it is as if Jesus has taken the "scorecard" and completely rubbed out all our mistakes, failures, and character flaws. The scorecard is clean. But then he went further by taking that scorecard and "nailed it to the cross." The scorecard was actually not just nailed to the cross; it was nailed *into Jesus himself.* Jesus took upon himself all of our mistakes, failures, and character flaws.

King Jesus disarmed all the powers that hold us down. Because King Jesus took all our failures on himself, he has "disarmed" the weapons of the powers that keep us down. Unfortunately, the evil one still tries to hold various weapons to our heads, but Jesus has taken upon himself all the bullets from Satan's weapons, and now he is shooting us with blanks! What are the "weapons" of the destructive powers in our lives? The first is *shame.* Shame is one of the most destructive powers, not only in the various shame cultures of the world, but also in our daily lives in the West. But Jesus has disarmed the weapon of shame. God himself has stepped in and taken the blame for all the mistakes you have made, and so no one can accuse you any longer. Now the truth can be told about our lives; we can come out in the open and admit our failures because there is no one that can accuse us. "If God is for us, who can be against us?" (Rom. 8:31). *And God is for you!* You can get past your past because God has taken upon himself your shame and replaced it with love and with a community of people who are just like you—sinners saved by God's love.

Another weapon that King Jesus has disarmed is *fear.* Not only has our shame led us to live fearful lives, but so many things make us anxious today. King Jesus has disarmed the power of anxiety and fear. "God, who did not spare his own Son, but gave him up for us all—how will he not also, along with him, graciously give us all things?" (Rom. 8:32). God's "gracing" us with forgiveness is just the beginning of a lifelong love relationship with him, where we learn to trust that he will care for us in everything in life. Nothing can separate us from the love of God—not death nor sufferings in life, not the present difficulties nor an uncertain future, *nor any powers* can separate us from the love of God in King Jesus our Lord (Rom. 8:38). Love has taught me not to fear because I hold the nail-scarred hands of King Jesus.

King Jesus invites us to join in the Parade of Life. Paul uses another powerful picture to depict all that King Jesus has done for us: he says that King Jesus has made a "public spectacle of the powers, triumphing over them by the cross." Paul is alluding to the victory parade of triumphant Roman emperors. Whenever Rome would defeat a warring city, they would take all the treasures of the defeated city along with the defeated king of the city and bring them back to Rome. Then they would have a big parade through the streets of Rome, and people would line up for miles to see the victory parade. First came the Roman soldiers carrying the treasures they captured. Next came the defeated king and his family and entourage, making them a "public spectacle" and humiliating them with the defeat. Last came the Roman emperor in all his glory, the victorious king. That is the picture of what King Jesus has done for us. He has captured us with his love and forgiveness because he treasures us. We are no longer enslaved to the powers that hold us down; we belong to the love of God, our new King. By doing this, King Jesus has publicly shamed Satan and all the powers that accuse us and make us fearful. King Jesus invites us to join him, the victorious King, in the victory parade of life, no longer enslaved to shame, fear, worry, regret, bitterness, anger, or any other power that no longer has power over us.

The Cross is the site of God's forever victory. The place where God was victorious, the cross, is such a beautiful, ironic paradox. But that is how love works: it takes the place of shame and makes it something gloriously beautiful. As McKnight writes, "the ultimate paradox is now clear: the location to celebrate victory is not the Roman forum or the public streets of Roman cities, but instead the precise place where Rome thought it was dominant: the cross. The powers are reversed: at the place where Rome used as the ultimate indignity, God reestablishes the dignity of all. Jesus himself was stripped, and

Jesus both was conquered and conquered at the cross."[1] As N.T. Wright says, "the cross was not the defeat of Christ at the hands of the powers; it was the defeat of the powers at the hands—yes, the bleeding hands—of Christ."[2]

†

King Jesus, the Lord of all the earth and the One who has dethroned and disarmed all the powers of our destructive culture and those in my life. I praise you for fighting with your own life all the dark powers of this world. I praise you for letting all the evil, hate, and lies of the world take out all their fury on you, exhausting their power. I praise you that I no longer need to live in shame or fear. I praise you that I am joining the victory parade of Jesus and am going to live my life helping others join, too. Praise your name, victorious King Jesus!

---

[1]McKnight, 260.
[2]N.T. Wright, *Following Jesus: Biblical Reflections on Discipleship* (Grand Rapids, MI: Eerdmans, 1994), 19.

DON'T LOSE CONNECTION WITH THE HEAD

Therefore do not let anyone judge you by what you eat or drink, or with regard to a religious festival, a New Moon celebration or a Sabbath day. 17 These are a shadow of the things that were to come; the reality, however, is found in Christ. 18 Do not let anyone who delights in false humility and the worship of angels disqualify you. Such a person also goes into great detail about what they have seen; they are puffed up with idle notions by their unspiritual mind. 19 They have lost connection with the head, from whom the whole body, supported and held together by its ligaments and sinews, grows as God causes it to grow. (2:16-19)

Speaking the truth in love, we will grow to become in every respect the mature body of him who is the head, that is, Christ. From him the whole body, joined and held together by every supporting ligament, grows and builds itself up in love, as each part does its work. (Eph. 4:15-16)

This passage begins with words we all need to hear: "Do not let anyone judge you." Unfortunately, we live in a *very judgmental* world—a "cancel culture." Although the church gets a bad rap for being judgmental, that charge is hypocritical because *everyone is judgmental.* There are legalists in the world, just like there are legalists in the church. Our modern world is filled with all kinds of good causes and "fights against injustice." But so often the fight for justice can turn into just a fight, and justice is pursued in very unjust ways. As philosopher Charles Taylor notes, our pursuit of justice can sometimes be "fueled by hatred" and "fed by our sense of superiority."[1] How can we seek justice without becoming unjust? Taylor says only unconditional love for every person can temper, control, and ultimately motivate our desire for good causes.[2]

Jesus said that we have to make judgments in life, but he showed us how to judge correctly: with grace. Jesus said that we should first take the huge plank out of our own eye (Matt. 7:5). When we have gone through that process (looking first at our faults and addressing them), then we will be able to see more clearly how to help someone else take the speck of dust out of their eye. The message for Christians is: don't let the world judge you for the truth of God, but speak the truth to others in the same way Jesus spoke truth: in love. Or as Paul would later say in Colossians, "Let your conversation always be full of grace, seasoned with salt, so that you may know how to answer everyone" (4:6).

The passage also gives us a clearer picture of what Paul and Timothy were combating. As Paul lays out exactly what the false teachers were teaching, he counters their teaching with the positive focus of King Jesus:

The False Teaching: The false teachers were saying that to be spiritual and attain a heightened spirituality, people must observe the Jewish ceremonial laws and practice strict discipline. As we have seen, these practices included dietary restrictions,

---

[1]Taylor, *A Secular Age*, 697.
[2]Id, 697-98.

celebrating Jewish religious festivals, and strict Sabbath observance.

The Positive Counter: These Old Testament ceremonial laws were symbols, foreshadowing the reality that came in King Jesus. The animal sacrifices and Jewish festivals (as well as all of the Torah) find their true fulfillment in what Jesus has now done for us.

The False Teaching: The false teachers were claiming that heightened spiritual experiences are the goal of religion, and they knew how to attain such mystical experiences. The phrase "worship of angels" probably refers to participating with angels in worship, or "angel-like worship."[3] The "false humility" probably refers to the "austere ascetic practices as a portal into mystical experiences that generate moral superiority and perhaps even divine revelation."[4] These false teachers were saying that they knew how to help one "worship with the angels," and all of their discipline and techniques could lead one into self-induced mystical experiences (which sounds a little like Eastern and new age mysticism). But because spiritual experiences were their goal, they had become "puffed up" and filled with pride. It doesn't take long for such pride to result in jealousy and conflicts in any group of people where self-gratifying experiences are the goal.

The Positive Counter: Paul says they have lost connection with "the head." The head is King Jesus himself, and Jesus as the head means he is the source of all true spiritual experiences. The goal of the mystical religions of the world is personal happiness, and those who pursue such mystical experiences for selfish reasons will end up disillusioned. The true "source" of the deepest spiritual experiences is King Jesus, the crucified one who is a servant for others. Pride and being "puffed up"

---

[3]See McKnight, 276-277.

[4]Id, 276.

have no place at the cross. Instead of seeking mystical experiences to achieve our own personal happiness, we need to be connected with the suffering Servant and join him in serving others. Paul uses the word "head" here to refer to Jesus to make this point: when we see the Servant King Jesus as the head of his body, then we join in that body (the community of his church) and Jesus teaches us how to love others like he loves us. Instead of pride and self-gratifying worship, the church of Jesus is an organic body whose members depend on and serve each other. We certainly worship with all of our might! But we worship because in Jesus, we see both Truth and Grace. He has rescued us from our past and provides meaning and purpose for our future and forever. He is the one who has done all this through his selfless, sacrificial love. We can't help but worship!

Unfortunately, history is replete with examples of churches that have taken their focus off Jesus and placed it on something else, even things as important as church growth, preaching, worship, mission efforts, and even losing weight. As Matt Redman's song says, "I'm coming back to the heart of worship, and it's all about you, Jesus."[5] Any church that takes its constant focus off King Jesus as the source for unity and everything God gives us will veer into some fad or trend that will ultimately lead to pride and division. In whatever we do as a church, we need to constantly ask: Is this highlighting Jesus, who he is, and all that he has done?

†

Praise you, Lord Jesus, that you bring together so coherently and beautifully all I can know about God. Everything about you centers and aligns us to truth: your teaching, your selflessness, your suffering with

[5]Matt Redman, "The Heart of Worship," Capitol CMG Publishing.

and for us, and your resurrection from the dead! Help me to constantly keep my focus on you. Lord Jesus, may your words from the Gospels become ingrained in me so that I truly become an apprentice of yours. Thank you, King Jesus, for teaching me how to become human again. I love you!

HOW TO BECOME THE HUMAN YOU WANT TO BE

> *Since you died with Christ to the elemental spiritual forces of this world, why, as though you still belonged to the world, do you submit to its rules: 21 "Do not handle! Do not taste! Do not touch!"? 22 These rules, which have to do with things that are all destined to perish with use, are based on merely human commands and teachings. 23 Such regulations indeed have an appearance of wisdom, with their self-imposed worship, their false humility and their harsh treatment of the body, but they lack any value in restraining sensual indulgence. (2:20-23)*

Paul is going to pivot now from combatting false teaching to a better way (the only way) to become the human God created you to be. A Bible word to describe all that we want to become as humans is the word "holy" (same word used to describe the "saints," or people made holy by God). In a sense, holy means "whole." Wholeness is what we long for as humans; we want a *cohesive* life, one in which all our desires, emotions, habits, and relationships come together into a unified, meaningful whole. We want our lives to have purpose, our relationships to be rich, our loves to be pure and enduring. And why wouldn't we—that is how God created us to be. How do we become *whole?*

Willpower alone cannot change us. As Paul said, "Do this!" and "Don't do that!" have an appearance of wisdom, but they really can't change us. As we all have experienced, "Just say no!" doesn't work. We live from the depths; our actions spring from who we are, from our "character." So how is character formed, and how do we become the "characters" we so very much long to become?

This passage is part of one long passage (2:16 through 3:17) where Paul and Timothy will explain in practical detail how we can become the people we most want to become. But to understand how this transformation occurs, we first have to understand the components that make up the people we are, what you might call the "parts of your human self." Paul will refer to these parts of our self as "members of our bodies" in Romans 6:13 and Col. 3:5.

The Parts of our Human Self

Every one of us has certain aspects or parts of ourselves that make up who we are. These consist of:

- *Our Will/Heart/Spirit:* We all have the ability to make choices—that is part of what makes us human. You could call this ability to choose our "will." Two Bible words for our "will" are heart and spirit. The Bible word for "heart" includes not only our will, but our emotions and our minds. It is the center of who we are, the "CEO" of all of our decision-making. As the Bible emphasizes, if you get the "heart" right, everything else will follow (Luke 7:21). And our hearts are driven by what we love, what we cherish and "treasure." As Jesus said, "Where your treasure is, there your heart will be also" (Matt. 6:21).

- *Our Mind:* How we think and what we think about powerfully affect who we are and what we do. We desperately need "mental health," which means taking care of our minds by how we think about ourselves, our world, and reality. Our minds are also beautifully equipped to help us harness our emotions. Our emotions serve the beautiful purpose of warning and alerting us to things around us, but unless we harness our emotions with our minds, they can consume us. "Feelings are…good servants. But they are disastrous masters."[1]

- *Our Body:* Our physical bodies are part of who we are, and we do a great disservice to ourselves when we try to separate our bodies from "who we are." Our bodies also greatly influence what we do. If we aren't getting good sleep, we have less control over our emotions. Addicts know that they should not let themselves become tired or hungry because when they do, their defenses are down. Similarly, what we repeatedly do with our bodies shapes the kind of people we become. Our bodies are composed of chemicals and neurons; the more we do a certain destructive thing (such as fill our bodies with destructive chemicals or pornographic images), the more addicted we become to those chemicals or images. Conversely, if we repeatedly do positive things with our bodies, our bodies change in positive ways. Scientists tell us that we have the power to physically change the neuron pathways in our brains by what we think about and what we do. "When people consistently make choices about their patterns of behavior, physical

[1]Dallas Willard, *Renovation of the Heart: Putting on the Character of Christ* (Colorado Springs, CO: NavPress, 2002), 122.

changes take place within the brain itself…choices you make about how you behave create new information pathways and patterns in your brain."[2] In other words, our bodies can be great servants, but they can also be horrible masters.

- *Our Social Environment:* Humans are social creatures—we desperately need other people in our lives. And our social environment also greatly affects the kind of people we become. Many of our problems as humans stem from the destructive relationships we have had in the past (maybe even the family we grew up in) or from hurtful and harmful relationships we are in. To become the people we most want to become, all of us need to be in nurturing, loving relationships where we not only receive love, but we give and love others in return.

The Process of Becoming the Person We Most Want to Become

The late Christian philosopher Dallas Willard did a masterful job at helping us understand who we are and how we change as humans. Below is a diagram that Willard prepared that helps us understand ourselves better:[3]

[2]Wright, "Why Christian Character Matters," in *All Things Hold Together in Christ*, 164; see also John Medina, *Brain Rules* (Seattle: Pear, 2008);

[3]See Willard, *Renovation of the Heart*, 38.

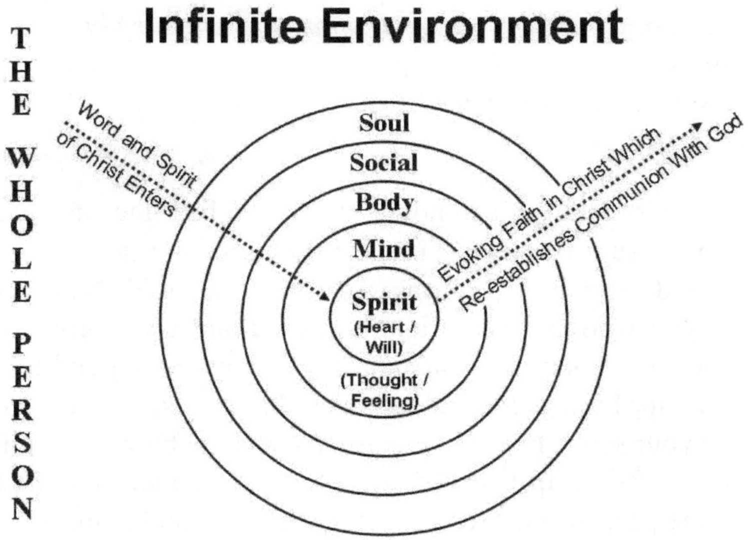

Dallas Willard said the process of becoming the person we most want to become, what we might call *spiritual formation*, is not complicated.

> Spiritual formation is not about behavior modification. It is about changing the sources of behavior, so the behavior will take care of itself. When the mind is right and the heart is right and the body and the soul and the relationships that we have in our social world are right, the whole person simply steps into the way of Christ and lives there with joy and strength. It is not a struggle.[4]

Paul put it this way:

---

[4]Dallas Willard, *Living in Christ's Presence: Final Words on Heaven and the Kingdom of God* (Downers Grove, Il: Intervarsity Press, 2014), 14.

> *Offer every part of yourself (literally, every "member of your body") to King Jesus as an instrument of righteousness. For sin shall no longer be your master because you are not under law but under grace. (Rom. 6:13, 14)*

Spiritual formation is also not hard; it is, in fact, the easy way, the restful way. It is *going with the grain* of the universe because God created us this way. As King Jesus said, "Come to me all you who are weary and burdened and I will give you rest. Take my yoke [my teaching/training] upon you and learn from me, for I am gentle and humble in heart, and you will find rest for your souls. For my yoke is easy and my burden is light" (Matt. 11:28-30). In Col. 3:5 and Rom. 6:13, Paul tells us to "offer the parts of yourselves" under the love and authority of King Jesus and to change your "masters." We are no longer under the "masters" of addiction, our past, our fears, our emotions, destructive relationships, or our selfishness. We have a new Master who loves us, knows who we are and how best to live, and we have put ourselves under his protection, love, and authority. As we do that, Paul says, "the benefit you reap leads to *holiness* and the result is eternal life" (Rom. 6:22).

As we will see later, this process of spiritual formation begins when we are seized by the power of God's Great Affection for us and when we realize we don't have to live our lives following the dead-end narratives of this world. Change begins when we realize there is a better love helping us to a better way to live.

†

> *Lord Jesus, I praise you that you show me how to become a whole, thriving human. I want to be an apprentice of yours, looking at your life. But even more, I want*

to be trained by you to become the person I most want to become. I surrender the parts of myself—my will, my mind, my body, my emotions, my relationships—over to you and to your Lordship. I know this will take time, but I praise you for never giving up on me. Thank you for showing me what real love is and making me whole. I love you!

WALKING HABIT: TAKE CARE OF YOUR BODY

A critical part of "spiritual" formation is taking care of your body. As James Bryan Smith writes, "Our bodies and souls are unified. If our bodies suffer, so do our souls. We cannot neglect the body in pursuit of spiritual growth. In fact, neglecting our bodies necessarily impedes our spiritual growth."[5] Some practical and necessary ways to take care of our bodies are:

- *Exercise.* Take a long, relaxing walk in nature as many times as possible during the week.
- *Begin eating more healthy foods.*
- *Sleep.* Sleep is one of the most important things we can do for our health (7-8 hours/night). One way to improve your sleep is to completely unplug an hour before bed—no screen time or social media.[6]

---

[5]James Bryan Smith, *The Good and Beautiful God*, 34.

[6]To explore the benefits of sleep, see Peter Attia, M.D., with Bill Gifford, *Outlive: The Science and Art of Longevity* (New York: Harmony, 2023).

A NEW LOVE AND A NEW STORY

Since, then, you have been raised with Christ, set your hearts on things above [seek the things above], where Christ is, seated at the right hand of God. 2 Set your minds on things above, not on earthly things. 3 For you died, and your life is now hidden with Christ in God. 4 When Christ, who is your life, appears, then you also will appear with him in glory. (3:1-4)

For in Christ, all the fullness of God lives in bodily form, and in Christ you have been brought to fullness (2:9,10).

Because of his great love for us, God, who is rich in mercy, made us alive with Christ even when we were dead in transgressions—it is by grace you have been saved. And God raised us up with Christ and seated us with him in the heavenly realms in Christ Jesus, in order that in the coming ages he might show the incomparable riches of his grace, expressed in his kindness to us in Christ Jesus. (Eph. 2:4-7)

Paul grabs our attention by helping us realize again how completely King Jesus has changed everything. King Jesus came to this earth for the sole purpose of rescuing us, raising us up, and bringing us back to become the humans he created us to be in the first place. And just as King Jesus is now over all the "powers," he has also raised us up *now* to have his heavenly vantage point over everything in life and in death. What Paul says here and in Ephesians 2:4-7 is that we are now, *presently*, raised with Christ in the heavenly realm. It is not just that someday we will be with Jesus forever in the new creation (which is our certain hope); Jesus has raised us up to be with him *now*. We have already been transferred into his Kingdom, protection, power, and authority: "He has rescued us from the dominion of darkness and brought us into the kingdom of the Son he loves, in whom we have redemption, the forgiveness of sins" (Col. 1:13).

A New Love

The writer Frederick Buechner once wrote, "I think maybe it is holiness that we long for more than we long for anything else."[1] As we saw previously, in one sense holiness means "wholeness." But the origin of the word "holy" is interesting. The word holy comes from pagan and Jewish temple practices, and it literally means taking something that was common (like a cup) and using it for sacred purposes in temple worship. The ordinary cup becomes "special" or sacred because of what it is dedicated or devoted to. In pagan worship, the cup was devoted to an "idol," or a substitute for God. In contrast, in Jewish worship the cup was devoted to the one true God, and by being dedicated to God, the cup became "holy."

The same thing happens to us. All of us are dedicated or devoted to something in life, and usually, we devote ourselves to what we think will bring us the things we most desire, our

[1]Frederick Buechner, *Secrets in the Dark* (New York: HarperOne, 2006), 242.

"treasures." Jesus was right (as he always is): "Where your treasure is, there your heart will be also" (Matt. 6:21). Whatever we love is like a weight or magnet, pulling our lives toward it. Augustine said that all evil comes from *disordered loves*. Those things that we love, that we have set our affections on, can twist us so that our lives become twisted, disordered. There are hundreds of examples of this in our lives, ranging from a disordered love of money, success, fame, acceptance, work, pleasure, addictions, even a disordered love of family or friends. The Bible's word for this twisted love is *idolatry*. Although we think these idols and loves will bring us the deep-down wholeness we are after, the problem with them is that they fail, in themselves, to bring us what we want. The Old Testament would often say that when people worshipped worthless idols, they became worthless themselves (Jer. 2:5). Instead of helping us become the humans we most want to be, these false idols can dehumanize us. When people give their hearts to these idols,

> …it is inevitable that their lives will be deformed in the image of the idol. Remade in the image and likeness of our own handiwork, we are revealed as commodities. Idolatry exacts its full price from us. We are robbed of our very humanity.[2]

Jesus is the flip side of idolatry. We are captured by God's great love for us, and we respond by giving our hearts totally to King Jesus. By devoting ourselves to him and his love, we actually become the humans we most want to be. As G.K. Beale writes, "People will always reflect something, whether it be God's character or some feature of the world. If people are

---

[2]Walsh and Keesmaat, 163, quoting John Francis Kavanaugh, *Following Christ in a Consumer Society: The Spirituality of Cultural Resistance* (Maryknoll, N.Y.: Orbis, 1981), 26.

committed to God, they will become like him; if they are committed to something other than God, they will become like that thing, always spiritually inanimate and empty like the lifeless and vain aspect of creation to which they have committed themselves."[3] Jesus is our escape from the grip of the idols that control us. How do we escape the grip of addiction and those things that twist our souls? The power of a Greater Love, the allure of a Greater Affection. "Only one thing can turn us away from what we love: a greater love."[4] We cannot just remove our idols; we must replace them, and we replace them with the in-flowing and over-flowing Love of God. The Love of God is the greatest affection you will ever experience; the sacrificial, unconditional love of God displayed on the cross of Jesus can now be poured into your heart through the very Spirit of God, and you can begin experiencing the height, depth, width and length of the Love of God (Rom. 5:5: Eph. 3:21ff).

A New Story

All of us live our lives as part of one or more stories. Our story may be to have a successful career, or be known for making money or for doing something well. Our story may be to have children and raise a large family. We all live inside "stories," ways we think about our lives and how we want them to turn out. Our stories dictate what we value, and what we value dictates how we live. Christian philosopher Alasdair MacIntyre put it this way: "I can only answer the question 'What am I to do?' if I can answer the prior question 'Of what story or stories

---

[3]G.K. Beale, *We Become What We Worship: A Biblical Theology of Idolatry* (Downers Grove, Il.: InterVarsity Press, 2008), 284.
[4]Peter Kreeft, *The God Who Loves You* (San Francisco: Ignatius Press, 1988), 123.

do I find myself a part?'"[5] The way we act, our ethics and daily practices, come out of who we are (our character), but our character is formed by what *story* we see ourselves in.

What story do you see yourself in? The story of Jesus is a real story—Jesus actually lived at one time in human history, part of a very historical (and enduring) people, the Jews. Jesus also actually died a purposeful death and was resurrected from the dead with an indestructible body. This is a real, historical story. But the "realness" of it is how the story changes everything, and how it has changed human lives and human culture dramatically over the last 2,000 years. In this passage, Paul helps us locate ourselves in *the metanarrative* ("big picture" narrative) of King Jesus, and this metanarrative is the fulfillment of the long Jewish narrative of how God has been with humans throughout history. King Jesus is the central character in God's interactions with humans, the culmination of God's story. That also means *our story*, the narrative of our life, has changed drastically. We now know where we have been, why we are here, and where we are going.

The Greatest Story Ever

The metanarrative of King Jesus is the greatest story ever and the antidote to our postmodern aimlessness. Our world today is skeptical of the stories they have been told, and for good reason. But this skepticism and "deconstruction" has left us with nothing—no good and enduring metanarrative. Because of this, people experience what sociologist David Lyon calls "the vertigo of relativity" and the "abyss of uncertainty."[6] The post-

[5]Alisdair McIntyre, *After Virtue: A Study of Moral Theory*, 2nd ed. (Notre Dame, Ind.: University of Notre Dame Press, 1984), 216.
[6]David Lyon, *Postmodernity* (Minneapolis: University of Minnesota Press, 1994), 61.

modern world of individual choice, consumer preference, distrust and pluralism "creates a heady cocktail that seems quickly to befuddle and paralyze."[7]

But God has given us a metanarrative, the greatest story ever--the King Jesus Story. It is the story of the Great Spirit, the Creator of the universe, making himself known to us in a way we can understand. The story says that long before the Creator created everything, he had us humans in mind, and in fact, we were created in the image of the prototype for humanity, God the Son. God created us in love, to love, and to enjoy love, and he created us to be with other humans in community, reflecting the "community" of God himself. Because he is love, he didn't create us as robots but as free creatures, able to respond or not respond to his love. Instead of becoming all God created us to be (gloriously, loving humans), we have chosen selfishly and fearfully to be our own gods, devoted to treasures that only destroy and divide us. But even before he created us, God already had in place the plan to rescue and restore us to reflect the image of God the Son. The cross was not an afterthought—God planned it even before he created the world. King Jesus has come to rescue us from everything that destroys us, even death.

The King Jesus Story changes not just how we view death, but how we view life. When Paul says, "seek the things above, where King Jesus is seated at the right hand of God," he is not saying "think about heaven and where you will be someday." Instead, he is saying "Set your hearts on and allow your imagination to be liberated to comprehend Christ's legitimate rule," and "Allow your vision of life, your worldview, your most basic life orientation, to be directed by Christ's heavenly rule at the right hand of God."[8] As Walsh and Keesmaat note, "Seeking that which is above is a matter not of becoming heavenly

[7]Lyon, 64-65.
[8]Walsh and Keesmaat, 155.

minded, but of allowing the liberating rule of Christ to transform every dimension of your life."[9] Tomorrow we will begin to see how King Jesus can transform every dimension of our lives.

†

King Jesus, you have captivated me by your love. Your love has reached into my heart and assured me that there is a God and that you, God, are filled with love for me. Your love has assured me that there is a purpose to humanity and history, and that you are involved particularly in my story. My story is going somewhere because you are with me. I can trust you because of Jesus, and today I give you my loves and my story. Thank you, Almighty Father and King Jesus, for loving me.

[9]Walsh and Keesmaat, 155.

A NEW WAY OF THINKING

Set your minds on things above, not on earthly things. 3 For you died, and your life is now hidden with Christ in God. 4 When Christ, who is your life, appears, then you also will appear with him in glory….Put on the new self, which is being renewed in knowledge in the image of its Creator…Let the message of Christ dwell among you richly as you teach and admonish one another with all wisdom through psalms, hymns, and songs from the Spirit, singing to God with gratitude in your hearts. (3:2-4, 10, 16)

Put off the old self, which is being corrupted by its deceitful desires, and be made new in the attitude of your minds, and put on the new self, created to be like God in true righteousness and holiness. (Eph. 4:23, 24)

After Paul tells us to seek the things of King Jesus (a new love and a new story), he immediately says, "set your mind on things above." He does this because what we think about dramatically shapes who we become, either for good or for bad. Both Jesus and Paul consistently emphasized that how we think and what we think about is the beginning point in changing us into the people we most want to become. Jesus said the greatest commandment is "Love God with all your heart, soul, *mind*, and strength, and love your neighbor as yourself" (Mark

12:30). For Jesus (and the Hebrews), there was no difference between heart and mind. The heart (our will and spirit) is strongly influenced by what we think, and conversely, we can decide (by what is in our hearts) how we think. Paul made it clear how important it is to change the way we think and to consistently bring before our minds better thoughts that ring true with reality. Listen to what Paul tells us:

> *Don't copy the behavior and customs of this world, but let God transform you into a new person by changing the way you think. Then you will learn to know God's will for you, which is good and pleasing and perfect . (Rom. 12:2, NLT)*

> *Those who are dominated by the sinful nature think about sinful things, but those who are controlled by the Holy Spirit think about things that please the Spirit. So letting your sinful nature control your mind leads to death. But letting the Spirit control your mind leads to life and peace. (Rom. 8:5,6, NLT)*

> *Fix your thoughts on what is true, and honorable, and right, and pure, and lovely, and admirable. Think about things that are excellent and worthy of praise. (Phil. 4:8, NLT)*

The Scriptures are filled with exhortations for humans to let the Word of God fill, shape, and expand our minds for our own benefit. The way of God, which we must learn with our minds, is the way of blessing, happiness, and life (see Ps. 19:17ff). As Willard writes,

> …as we first turned away from God in our thoughts, so it is in our thoughts that the first movements toward

> renovation of the heart occurs. Thoughts are the place where we can and must begin to change…The ultimate freedom we have as human beings is the power to select what we allow or require our minds to dwell upon.[1]

What Does it Mean to Think About Things Above?

What Paul says here wasn't confusing to him or his readers, but it can be for us. When Paul says, "Think of things above, where Christ is," he doesn't mean think about how it will be in heaven someday or think about some amorphous and vague idea of Jesus sitting on the clouds. " 'To set one's mind on things above' does not mean to 'think about heaven,' but to orient one's life and devotion to God rather than to the self or the world…[Paul] does not view new life in Christ as withdrawal from this earth or turning away from concern for life here on this earth; quite the contrary. 'The things above' are those values, desires, and behaviors that reflect Christ's supremacy over the cosmos, hence deriving their orientation and value from him."[2] As McKnight writes, "Far from a summons to an un- or otherworldliness, this exhortation calls the Colossians to live in the world *on the basis of the rule of Christ over the powers*" (emphasis his).[3] And this is done by daily saturating ourselves with words from God—letting God speak to you through the Scriptures. "Let the word of Christ dwell in you richly" (3:16). By reading this book, you are doing that!

---

[1]Willard, *Renovation of the Heart*, 95.
[2]Thompson, 71.
[3]McKnight, 290.

Let me give you some further encouragement for today from Dallas Willard:

> I constantly and thoughtfully engage myself with the ideas, images, and information that are provided by God through the Scriptures, his Son Jesus… In doing that, I am constantly nourished by the Holy Spirit in ways far beyond my own efforts or understanding. This has special importance when I am faced with the presence of evil and suffering in human life. I realize that I will either allow my view of evil to determine my view of God and will cut him down accordingly, or I will allow my view of God to determine my view of evil and will elevate him accordingly, accepting that nothing is beyond his power for good.[4]
>
> If we allow everything access to our mind, we are simply asking to be kept in a state of mental turmoil or bondage. For nothing enters the mind without having an effect of good or evil.[5]

†

Father God, King Jesus, and the Spirit of Truth, thank you for my mind. Thank you, especially, for ordering my mind by speaking to me. Thank you for giving me mental health as I let your Word indwell me. Your Word brings order, love, reason, practical wisdom, endurance, comfort, and hope. Thank you for speaking to me through your Word, which reveals so beautifully your true Word to us, my King Jesus. Let your Word dwell in me richly today.

---

[4]Willard, *Renovation of the Heart*, 109.
[5]Willard, *Renovation of the Heart*, 111.

WALKING HABIT: LET THE WORD OF CHRIST DWELL IN YOU RICHLY

If you are not already in a daily Bible reading or listening plan, begin now. The Bible Recap (with Tara Leigh Coble) is an excellent place to start.[6] Another proven reading plan is to read one Psalm and one chapter from a Gospel each day. I would highly encourage you to always be reading in the Gospels. The beautiful Gospel of John is a great place to start. Become an apprentice of Jesus by watching him, listening to him, loving him, following him, imitating him. As Jesus prayed for us, "Make them holy for Yourself by the truth. Your Word is truth" (John 17:17).

[6]https://www.thebiblerecap.com/ .

NEW HABITS AND PRACTICES

> *Put to death, therefore, whatever belongs to your earthly nature: sexual immorality, impurity, lust, evil desires and greed, which is idolatry. 6 Because of these, the wrath of God is coming. 7 You used to walk in these ways, in the life you once lived. (3:5-7)*

Paul continues to give us practical advice on how we can become the people we most want to become by talking about our *habits*. What we do shapes our character--who we are--in ways we often fail to realize. Scientists tell us that the neuropathways in our brain change based on what we do as much as by what we think. The more we do a certain habit or practice, the easier it is to do that habit or practice and the harder it is to break that habit or practice. In other words, our bodies, like our emotions, are great servants but horrible masters. Paul is now going to talk specifically about our bodies and our habits. He uses the old Jewish term of "walking" to refer to our habits, what we do on a daily or weekly basis.

What is God's Wrath?

How we "walk" means what we do, and Paul is saying we used to have habits that destroyed us. He says because of these, the "wrath of God is coming." When we read the words "wrath of

God," we immediately think of God having uncontrolled anger or punishing us. Far from the truth! In the Bible, the wrath of God is his settled will to bring about the best for us; he is against evil because it destroys us! God warns us in so many ways: through our conscience, through others, through circumstances, through his Word. Finally, he gives us the most severe warning by letting us reap the consequences of our actions. That is what the "wrath of God" means: letting us experience the painful consequences of going against his good will, against the grain of the universe. In Romans 1:18ff, Paul says, "the wrath of God is being revealed" as God "turns people over" to their own selfish desires and its consequences. "The wrath of God is simply the rule of the universe that a man will sow what he reaps and that one never escapes the consequences of his sin."[1] But we must also remember that the wrath of God includes his passionate, jealous love for us. The "rule of the universe" is actually the passionate love of God for humans. Only his ways are right and true because he is the Source of all that is good and right and true. But instead of letting us turn from that Source, God fights tooth and nail to bring us back. And part of bringing us back is letting us experience the consequences in the hope that we return. And when we do, we find he is rushing to meet us with outstretched, nail-scarred hands.

Greedy Habits of Selfishness

The particular habits Paul mentions in this passage that destroy us all have one thing in common: they reveal our *greediness*. The first four habits (sexual immorality, impurity, lust, and evil desires) have to do with sensual desires. But it is interesting how Paul here and in other places associates uncontrolled sen-

[1]William Barclay, *Colossians*, 152.

sual desires with *greed.* Paul makes the same connection in Ephesians 4:19 when he says those who turn from God "have lost all sensitivity, they have given themselves over to sensuality so as to indulge in every kind of impurity, and they are *full of greed.*" Jesus made the same connection (see Luke 16, Matthew 19, and Mark 10). The reason for this connection is because at bottom, uncontrolled sexual desire is just like greed: we seek to use another person to satisfy our own desires. Paul uses the term *porneia* for sexual immorality, from which we get the word pornography. Pornography is a billion-dollar business because it offers a quick way to satisfy our desires, and yet, like all distorted passions, it quickly turns into addiction, or to use the Bible word, idolatry. Pornography is at its base an abuse of ourselves and others because it distorts the beautiful gift of sexual intimacy. Sexual intimacy "is inseparable from a profound sense of giving, unity, openness, and therefore belonging. Any abuse of sexual intimacy is a uniquely evil affront against someone's personhood precisely because it treats that personhood as a means to an end."[2] Pornography destroys humans because it separates what God brought together. "Rather than bringing us closer to our humanity, it dehumanizes at every turn, turning our intimacy into instrumentality and leaving us addicted, depressed, exhausted, lonely, and bored—which also happens to be an accurate description of our society in general."[3]

So how do we break the cycle of greed, pornography, or any other dehumanizing addiction? Paul (and Jesus) tell us the two things that we must do.

---

[2]Noble, 66.
[3]Noble, 63, 64.

Put it to Death (Cut it Off)!

Paul tells us how we should deal with our dehumanizing habits. He doesn't say we should "work on them" or "keep an eye on them." He says bluntly, *kill them!* Suffocate them! Don't allow them to have any leeway or breath at all! Jesus bluntly says the same thing: "If your right hand causes you to sin, cut it off and throw it away!" (Matt. 5:30). What Jesus and Paul are saying is essentially what we would call today as *rehab:* getting away from any possibility of continuing the addictive behavior in a place where you simply cannot continue the behavior. A person with chemical addiction should rush immediately to a good rehab facility, preferably one with Christian-based counseling and therapy. Anyone addicted to any destructive habit needs to take drastic action to cut themselves completely off from any access to that destructive habit. You can't break a habit unless you stop doing it, and the first step to breaking a habit is admitting it is destructive and that you are powerless over your addiction. And not just admitting to yourself, but honestly confessing your addiction to another person. Confession breaks the power of addiction and is essential. These actions are the beginning steps of the Twelve Step Program (which is based on Bible teaching), which is historically the most successful substance abuse program. Our bodies and minds need time for healing, changing, and restoration, and unless we put those destructive habits to death, they will continue to destroy us. It is not enough to "put the wild animals of lust and hatred into cages: there they remain, alive and dangerous, a constant threat to their captor. Paul's solution is more drastic: the animals are to be killed."[4] If you are dealing with any addictive behavior, *now* is the time to put to death the thing that is killing you. You will need others to help you. Thankfully, there are many Christ-

---

[4]Wright, *Colossians*, 132.

inspired and Christ-based resources available—run and seek them out![5]

Start Training (Follow Me)!

We also have to replace bad habits with good habits. That means that we "walk" in the health-giving practices of God. Jesus put it simply, "Turn around, believe the Good News, and follow me" (Mark 1:15,17). Jesus is the Master on how to live flourishing lives, and we learn by being apprentices of his. His own Spirit, the Spirit of God, is our "coach" (the term Jesus uses in John 14-17 for the Holy Spirit, *paraclete*, can be translated as "coach"). Paul says in 1 Timothy 4:7, "Train yourself to be godly."

In order to change, we have to *train* spiritually just like we would train physically to get in shape. "To train means arranging our life around those practices that enable us to do what we cannot now do by direct effort. The point of training is to receive power, so we arrange our life around practices through which we receive power."[6] Physically, we can't just decide one day to run a marathon and be able to do it immediately. Instead, we train with various running exercises, and that training allows us, over time, to do what we cannot now do. It is the same with spiritual training. We simply must have daily practices to allow God to train us to think better, feel better, act better, love better. Such practices are often called *spiritual disciplines,* or what James Bryan Smith calls *soul-training exercises*.[7] These

---

[5]For example: Celebrate Recovery, https://www.celebraterecovery.com/; Renew, https://www.reneweveryday.com; Overcomers Outreach, https://overcomersoutreach.org/.

[6]Willard, *Living in Christ's Presence*, 140.

[7]James Bryan Smith, *The Good and Beautiful God*, 26.

are practices that allow God to train our hearts, minds, bodies, and emotions. These soul training exercises include:

Prayer
Solitude
Daily reading or listening to Scripture
Memorizing Scripture
Rest and practicing Sabbath
Giving and being more generous
Serving
Fasting
Confession
Sharing Communal Meals with other Christians
Practicing humility
Fellowship with other Christians
Sleep[8]

There are plenty of resources on spiritual disciplines and I highly recommend them.[9]

---

[8]Sleep doesn't seem like a spiritual discipline, but I believe it is one of the most neglected disciplines in our fast-paced world. For a discussion on the discipline of sleep, see James Bryan Smith, *The Good and Beautiful God*, 35.

[9]See, for example, Dallas Willard, *The Spirit of the Disciplines: Understanding How God Changes Lives* (New York: HarperCollins, 1988); Richard J. Foster, *Celebration of Discipline: The Path to Spiritual* Growth (New York: HarperCollins, 1978, 1988, 1998); Donald S. Whitney, *The Spiritual Disciplines of the Christian Life* (Colorado Springs, CO: NavPress, 1991, 2014); A. W. Tozer, *The Pursuit of God* (Waymark Books, 2020); John Mark Comer, *The Ruthless Elimination of Hurry: How to Stay Emotionally Healthy and Spiritually Alive in the Chaos of Modern Life* (Colorado Springs, CO: WaterBrook, 2019); *The Practice of the Presence of God*, by Brother Lawrence of the Resurrection (New York: Image Books, 1977); and James Bryan Smith, *The Good and Beautiful God: Falling in Love with the God Jesus Knows* (Downers Grove, Il: 2009).

†

Lord Jesus, whatever is in my life that is causing me destruction, I surrender it completely to you. You are my only hope, and you can rescue me and make something beautiful of my life. I praise you that you don't accuse or judge me; you love me and fight for me. Your love is the only way out, so fill me with your love and courage to take the next steps to let you change me. Lord Jesus, the Good Shepherd who lays down his life for me, thank you that you restore my soul and that you lead me in paths of righteousness. Thank you for preparing a feast in the presence of those enemies that are trying to destroy my soul. I will feast on your love instead of all the false loves that leave me empty and broken. Thank you for healing my brokenness.

WALKING HABIT: EXERCISE YOUR SOUL

Review the spiritual disciplines listed above. If there are any you are not currently practicing, start. Each of these training exercises are points of access to a deeper connection to the Spirit of God. Become an apprentice of King Jesus, and let him begin training your heart, mind, soul, and body to become the person you most want to become.

SOCIAL [MEDIA] SINS

But now you must also rid yourselves of all such things as these [put them all away]: anger, rage, malice, slander, and filthy language from your lips. 9 Do not lie to each other, since you have taken off your old self with its practices 10 and have put on the new self, which is being renewed in knowledge in the image of its Creator. 11 Here there is no Gentile or Jew, circumcised or uncircumcised, barbarian, Scythian, slave or free, but Christ is all, and is in all. (3:8-11)

Paul and Timothy turn their attention from "sins of greed" to actions and attitudes that are so prevalent in our society, all of which lead to the divisiveness and hate that fill our culture. As we have said throughout, to be human is to be *with others*. We find our "identity" by being part of a group. And our culture is filled with "identity politics," one group fighting against another, each talking past each other. The weapons in this fight are words, and the technology of this warfare is social media.

Finding our identity in a group makes us feel better, and attacking others through social media hardens us into silos. One hateful post is answered with an equally hateful post. Paul and Timothy are telling us we don't have to live like that anymore. That way of life is distorted, and that identity is not our true identity. What we need is to "put off" our old solidarity with any particular group (as worthy as we might think their causes are) and find our new solidarity and identity in the One who created us in the first place. King Jesus shows us through his sacrificial love how to be human and what makes for true peace. Paul and Timothy tell us to "put off" our old group solidarity and "put on" a new humanity, which is renewed in a new way of thinking and new practices.

To begin to do this, we need to realize how impactful our words and posts are. We are *responsible* for what we say and write, and the consequences of what we post are often so much worse than we intend. As Wright says, we cannot always prevent anger or hateful thoughts from coming into our heads, but we should search for creative ways of dealing with them because words

> …change situations and relationships, often irrevocably. Like wild plants blown by the wind, hateful words can scatter seeds far and wide, giving birth to more anger wherever they land.[1]

Paul and Timothy mention some of the actions and attitudes that we just need to *stop!* That means every time we are inclined to think a certain hateful or bitter way, or say (or write) words that inflame instead of heal, we need to *stop!* Paul and Timothy mention a few actions and attitudes we need to stop:

- *Anger (thumos) and rage (orge).* Anger is "slow-burning;" we let it simmer. Rage is sudden, but it springs from letting that anger simmer into a boil. The word for rage is *orge*, from which we get the English word orgy. Rage occurs when we let anger boil over, and we gorge ourselves on how bad we can make others feel.

[1]Wright, *Colossians*, 142.

- *Malice (kakia),* which means being "mean spirited" or "vicious."

- *Slander (blasphemia).* Interestingly, slander is the Greek word *blasphemia* from which we get the word blasphemy. We blaspheme God himself when we slander other people because all people are made in the image of God. We have no right to belittle or besmirch any other human being, no matter how much we disagree with them. All such belittling and slander should stop.

- *Filthy language.* A by-product of our divisive culture is how vulgar our language has become. Such vulgar language can act like a rocket to carry our hurtful payload. Ironically, vulgar language often uses the most intimate of human connections *intended for love* (sexual intercourse) and distorts it so that it instead becomes a missile intended to demoralize another. How the evil one has turned our whole humanity upside down!

- *Lying.* At the bottom of all of these is lying. We might call this "false information," and social media is filled with it. Although there might be some truth in what we post, we often distort the truth of what others say for our own agendas. "Truth is often inconvenient, untidy, or embarrassing, and we are constantly tempted to bend it into a less awkward shape."[2] Lying breeds mistrust and an environment where we are tempted to let hate be our defense.

---

[2]Id.

A New Community

But these all describe the old humanity, the old group in which we used to find our identity. We need to "put off" that old corporate group and "put on" (like a new set of clothes) a new community and new ways of thinking and acting. King Jesus has given us the image of what a human should be and act like, and he has shown us that we can become human when we are part of a completely "new humanity," a new community where sacrificial, forgiving love always triumphs over hate. Instead of hate being our defense, love is our defense because we have "put on" the reconciling love of King Jesus. His love *goes on the offense* to create new possibilities (not tied to the hate and bitterness of the past); new bonds (not the hate-filled allegiances of the world that divide us); and a new space, where all racial, ethnic, cultural, socio-economic, gender, and any other barrier or stereotype is broken down by the reconciling love of King Jesus.

Paul ends this passage by saying, "Here…." Where is "here?" Here is the same place he and Timothy have been describing throughout Colossians: "*in Christ (King Jesus).*" In Christ is the new space, the new protection and environment, where we can become human again. And to be "in Christ" means to be in "his body," the church, a new humanity where the walls that divide us come tumbling down. "Here" there are no stereotypes or divisions.

Paul and Timothy describe the barriers in the first century world that King Jesus broke through. "Here" Jews are no longer the chosen and holy people of God—God has called all of us as his chosen, dearly loved, and holy ones. Paul even mentions breaking down barriers that would have been unheard of in his day: slaves and free people worshipping together, free people serving slaves! "Barbarian" was a racial slur the Greeks used to describe foreigners because their language sounded like babbling ("bar-bar-bar"). But even the "barbarians" didn't associate with the "Scythians," which was a term used to describe those living north of the Black Sea in modern day southern Russian. Scythians were often thought of as the most barbaric of the barbarians. But here, in King Jesus, there are no "barbarians," no foreigners, no "educated or uneducated," no Republicans or Democrats, no Jews or Arabs, no divisions or stereotypes. We are all humans created in the image of God with dignity and worth, all being recreated by the reconciling, transforming love of King Jesus. "Here" is what the world sees and says, "that is what I want and need!"

†

King Jesus, thank you that my words have such an impact for healing and for good. But help me to realize that my words also have such an impact for hurt and that once spoken, they cannot be retrieved. Help me to be quick to listen, slow to speak, and slow to become angry. I thank you that I can learn from how patient you have been with me. Help me to remember to first take the huge log out of my eye before thinking about the specks in others' eyes. May my words today be full of grace, seasoned by your wisdom. I love you!

THE ARMOR OF LOVE

Therefore, as God's chosen people, holy and dearly loved, clothe yourselves with compassion, kindness, humility, gentleness and patience. 13 Bear with each other and forgive one another if any of you has a grievance against someone. Forgive as the Lord forgave you. 14 And over all these virtues put on love, which binds them all together in perfect unity. (3:12-14)

In these verses, Paul gives us a description of who we are as humans, where we find our true identity. We are *loved* by the God of the universe. *To be human is to be loved.* If we are not loved, and if we do not love others, we become less than human, which leads to dehumanizing behavior. Above all things, we as human beings find our identity, our peace and comfort, our meaning and purpose in life, by letting ourselves be loved by God. These words, "chosen, holy, and dearly loved" were the words God used to describe the people of Israel in the Old Testament (Ex. 19:5-6). But it was always his intention that every human being would hear God speaking these words to them—to you. And God has put his money where his mouth is by showing us how deep, wide, long, and high his love is by coming to be with us and to rescue us from all powers that hold us down, even death.

We understand what love is by looking at God as he has fully expressed himself in King Jesus. Love isn't a feeling, it is a "rugged commitment" to the well-being of another human being by being present with, fighting for, and sticking with another.[1] That kind of love is the only hope to overcome the selfishness that is in all of us, and we need Someone to stick with us and train us to love like that, too. That Someone is always on the cross for us, the cross that always leads to the triumph over our dark tombs.

Paul describes what love looks like in this passage, as if each description were a piece of clothing that we should visualize as being draped around Jesus. Then Jesus takes each piece of clothing and wraps it around us. We should also envision each of these as "pieces of armor" that are for our true protection. Hate is a defensive strategy; people hate because they are afraid, and they use hate to protect themselves. But hate doesn't protect your heart at all. Rather, it is like a sieve that lets in all the darkness that poisons your soul. What you need is the armor of love layered over you to protect you from a cold world. With this armor of love, you can be not just protected, but you can "go on the offense" and change relationships and life situations with each of these pieces of love. Another way to describe each of these is "fruit of the Spirit" (Gal. 5:22ff) which God spreads in our world through us. Here are the pieces of armor, the pieces of our new humanity, that we need to put on:

Compassion. Paul literally says that we should have the "bowels of compassion" (*splanchna oiktrimou*). We should feel for others from our gut. God is described as having this same compassion (2 Cor. 6:12, 7:15; Mark 1:41, 6:34). Another way to describe this is having a "heart of pity." Barclay notes that there was no mercy in the ancient world. Babies, animals, and sick people were all tossed aside. "Christianity brought mercy

---

[1]See McKnight, 93, 349.

into this world. It is not too much to say that everything that has been done for the aged, the sick, the weak in body and in mind, the animal, the child, the woman has been done under the inspiration of Christianity."[2] People are changed by compassion. Compassion is exactly what the world needs now.

Kindness. The Greek word for kindness is *chrestos*, which is a beautiful word because it is similar to Christ (*Christos*) and because it is derived from the Greek word for grace, *charis*. There is nothing more disarming than kindness; there is nothing that can change a situation, an environment, or a relationship like kindness. Kindness is so lacking in our culture, and Christians can change that culture by going on the "offensive" by being kind. People are changed when they are "graced" by kindness. Kindness is what the world needs now.

Humility. Christianity turned the world upside down when it revealed that God, the great and Almighty, was humble. In fact, God's greatness is shown in his utter humility to rescue us (Phil. 2:5ff). In the ancient world, humility was not a virtue; pride and arrogance were seen as virtues (resulting in the dehumanizing world of the ancients). "Humility was a virtue created by Christianity,"[3] and as David Brooks notes, "humility is the greatest virtue."[4] Humility is the greatest virtue because it forces us to see our own selfishness and opens the space for us to let others in, to let others grow and thrive. It is the opposite of the central vice, pride. God turned the ancient world upside down, and now, more than ever, we let God turn it upside down again by our kindness and humility. Humility is what the world needs now.

Gentleness/Meekness. The Greek word (*prautes*) can be translated as either gentle or meek, and it is used to describe

---

[2]William Barclay, 157.
[3]William Barclay, 158.
[4]Brooks, 263.

Jesus (2 Cor. 10:1) and Moses (Num. 12:3). Meekness is "strength under control." Followers of God can be gentle because they don't have to fret, worry, or be anxious about God taking care of them; it is the "meek" who will inherit the earth and all the blessings that God richly provides (see Ps. 37:11; Matt. 5:5). Gentleness is what the world needs now.

Patience. Patience (*makrothymia*) can be translated as "patient endurance" and "longsuffering." Patience is the beautiful character trait of God described in Exodus 34:5ff: "The LORD, the LORD God, merciful and gracious, longsuffering, and abounding in goodness and truth." The Hebrew word for "longsuffering" literally means "long of nose." Usually, when someone gets angry, their nose turns red. But God is "long of nose," meaning it takes a long time for his nose to turn red, and that is part of his grace to us. Because of God's patience, we can learn from our mistakes and turn back to him. In turn, our patience with others can bring about a change in their hearts and lives. Patience is what the world needs now.

Forgiveness. The Greek word used here, *charizomai*, literally means "gracing," or covering another person with grace. It means responding to hostility or anger with grace because that is how God has responded to us (Matt. 6:12, 14-15; Rom. 12:9-13:10). This is exactly why and how we can forgive: "Forgive (grace someone) as the Lord forgave you (graced you)." Forgiveness is what the world needs now.

The Coat of Love. Paul says that over all of these pieces of armor, "put on love, which binds them together in perfect unity." What is the motivation behind all of these virtues? Why do Christians live differently than the rest of the world? It is only because we have experienced the compassionate, humble, kind, gentle, patient, forgiving love of God in Jesus Christ. "We love because he first loved us" (1 John 4:19). What the world needs now is love.

†

Lord Jesus, thank you for wrapping me with your coat of love. God, I love you because of your compassion, kindness, humility, gentleness, patience, and forgiveness. Thank you that your love is the greatest defense in a hostile world. Your love has made me unafraid. Your love makes me confident to go on the offensive today and change my work environment, my family, all of my life situations by showing that same compassion, kindness, humility, gentleness, patience, and forgiveness. Thank you, Lord Jesus, that you teach us what love really is.

PEACE, SONG, AND THANKS

Let the peace of Christ rule in your hearts, since as members of one body you were called to peace. And be thankful. 16 Let the message of Christ dwell among you richly as you teach and admonish one another with all wisdom through psalms, hymns, and songs from the Spirit, singing to God with gratitude in your hearts. 17 And whatever you do, whether in word or deed, do it all in the name of the Lord Jesus, giving thanks to God the Father through him. (3:15-17)

Do not get drunk on wine, which leads to debauchery. Instead, be filled with the Spirit, 19 speaking to one another with psalms, hymns, and songs from the Spirit. Sing and make music from your heart to the Lord, 20 always giving thanks to God the Father for everything, in the name of our Lord Jesus Christ (Eph. 5:18-20)

The love of God expressed and confirmed in his coming to us in Jesus brings peace, peace in our hearts and peace among humans. This peace is not just an end to hostilities, it is the peace encompassed in the Hebrew word *shalom,* which means "flourishing," "well-being," "quiet confidence and rest." The peace that King Jesus has brought is the space for us to be at peace with God, with ourselves, with one another. God creates the space by his love for us so we can flourish, and we flourish as humans when we are part of the kind of community King Jesus creates. This is a community where others show us the self-sacrificing love of God, and where we in turn have the opportunity to mature as humans by loving and serving others. King Jesus, the Prince of Peace, brings hate and hostility to an end by taking upon himself all of our hate and hostility, and by showing us that the only way to break the grip of hate and bitterness is *his way*, the way of the cross. The way of Jesus takes the initiative to be a peacemaker. Jesus teaches us that in all our relationships, we need to be the first to say, "I'm sorry, I love you, let's reconcile." The creative love of God breaks down all barriers of hate, race, and culture, and creates the new space where humans can flourish in peace and love.

Paul says that this peace of King Jesus should "rule" in our hearts, both individually and in our community. The word Paul uses for "rule" (*brabeuto*) means "umpire." To say peace is the "umpire" means that "in making your decisions, in choosing between alternatives, in settling conflicts of will, a concern to preserve the inward and communal peace that Christ gave and gives should be your controlling principle."[1] Decisions should be made in such a way as to keep the unity of the Spirit through the bond of this peace, and that can only come about as each of us take on the mind of King Jesus, being "completely humble, gentle, patient, bearing with one another in love" (Eph. 4:2, 3).

The peace of Christ can permeate and rule (both in our hearts and in our churches) if we put into practice what Paul says next: "let the message about Christ dwell within you richly." The "you" here is plural, so that means the "word of Christ" should dwell richly both in our individual hearts and among us corporately as the body of Christ. The word (*logos*)

---

[1]Murray J. Harris, *Colossians and Philemon* (Nashville: B&H Academic, 2010), 165.

of Christ includes the Bible, through which God communicates to us and through which the Spirit illuminates our hearts and minds so that we may know God better (Eph. 1:17, 18). But the *logos* is also King Jesus himself, the full message and expression of God. As McKnight says, "the discussion is not so much about the Bible but what it says about Christ, whom the Bible serves and to whom the Bible points."[2]

For the message of King Jesus to dwell among us richly, we need to "grow up" in the way we think about the world and about all that God has done and is doing in Jesus. The Christian church has the beautiful answers to the division, confusion, and emptiness of our world in this 21st century. But those answers are not surface answers; they are deep and profound, and require all of us to think deeply, robustly, and *Christianly*. To address the serious challenges of our world, we simply must be better students of the Scriptures and take more of a Christ-focused approach to all the difficult issues that face our world. We need a *Christian anthropology*, a Christian understanding of what it means to be human.[3]

We do this individually, but we also do this when we are together, as *each of us* (not just our pastors, preachers, and teachers) brings a word about what God is doing in our lives. Interestingly, one important way God speaks to us and through us is through *song*. God created music, and there is something about music that allows the powerful message of Jesus to penetrate our hearts more than any sermon can. This is especially true when we are singing *together,* when we hear others singing at the top of their lungs about the greatness of God. When we

---

[2]McKnight, 330.

[3]Two fantastic references in this regard are *Humanity* by John S. Hammett and Katie J. McCoy (Brentwood, TN: B&H Academic, 2023), and John F. Kilner, *Dignity and Destiny: Humanity in the Image of God* (Grand Rapids, MI: Eerdmans, 2015).

sing together in the presence of God, we are singing *to God with others*: "it is the worship addressed to God with grateful hearts, from a community bound together by love and shaped by Christ's peace."[4]

Both the pathway to this peace and the result of Christ's peace is *thanksgiving*. It is not joy that brings gratitude; it is gratitude that brings joy in our hearts.[5] We need to give thanks to God constantly because being thankful delivers us from our bondage to fear and worry. Giving thanks reminds us of all that God has done so that we can remember that he is the one who can deliver us from our present situation. Giving thanks also brings contentment, which breaks us free from the grip and anxiety of greed. *God tells us to be thankful for our own good!*

†

Father God and King Jesus, you are worthy of all our worship. Creation cries out in worship to you through its beauty, vastness, and elegance. Our souls cry out in worship to you because of our deep-seated need for your Transcendence, for love, for meaning. We cry out to you because in you, we encounter the Transcendent and the Intimate, the Creator and Father God. And most especially, we encounter the God of our Lord Jesus Christ, who suffered with us and for us, releasing us from guilt, showing and teaching us what love is, and restoring us gently to become all that you created us to be. Set my heart ablaze with worship to you today! I commit to you today to spend time worshipping you, turning my attention from worthless things that make

---

[4]Thompson, 87.

[5]See David Steindl-Rast, *Gratefulness: The Heart of Prayer* (New York: Paulist Press/Ramsey, 1984), 204.

me worthless, and turning my full attention to the One who recalibrates my heart and soul with love, peace, confidence, and joy. I worship you, my Lord and King!

WALKING HABIT: WORSHIP

Humans were created to worship. If we do not worship the One True Creator God, we will worship "gods" that are *worth less* than our great God. And by worshipping things worth less than God, we will also become worthless (2 Kings 17:15). Worship centers our hearts and minds on the One who pulls us up and aligns us with all that is good, right, and true. Seek to worship every day. Put in earbuds, turn on Christian music, and sing at the top of your lungs! Read Psalms of praise out loud to God. Get alone and turn all your anxiety over to God because he cares for you. Go to church on Sunday, sing as loud as you can, and listen to the voices of others praising our great God and King. Be luxurious and extravagant in your worship of God. Make worship one of your most enjoyable habits!

NEW RULES OF THE HOUSE

Wives, submit yourselves to your husbands, as is fitting in the Lord. 19 Husbands, love your wives and do not be harsh with them. (3:18, 19)

Submit to one another out of reverence for Christ. Wives, submit yourselves to your own husbands as you do to the Lord... Husbands, love your wives, just as Christ loved the church and gave himself up for her...Each one of you also must love his wife as he loves himself, and the wife must respect her husband (Eph. 5:21, 22, 25, 33)

Paul and Timothy now take all they have said about King Jesus and address specifically the most intimate, and the most daily, of relationships: the home. Colossians 3:18-4:1 and Ephesians 5:21-6:9 are often referred to as "household codes" because they are patterned after the typical "household codes" written by Greek and Roman writers and philosophers. Aristotle in particular set down household codes that were to be the foundation and norm for Greek society.[1] Although this text is a "household code," what we need to see is how completely different and "upside down" this code is compared to Aristotle's. Just as King Jesus has lovingly but firmly subverted the power struc-

[1]Aristotle, *Politics.*

tures of the Roman Empire, King Jesus also subverts the ways we should think and act at home.

Aristotle's household code was based on the "proper ordering" of society and the home by what Aristotle said were the laws of nature. Accordingly, because Greeks were "naturally superior" to barbarians, the Greeks should rule. The same logic applied to masters over slaves, parents over children, and husbands over wives. Listen to why Aristotle said wives should submit to their husbands: "The male is by nature superior, and the female inferior; and the one rules, and the other is ruled; this principle of necessity extends to all mankind."[2] *In sharp contrast*, Paul (here in Colossians and in the companion text in Ephesians 5) challenges the person who is in power (the husband and father) "to turn that honor and power around for the good of the other."[3] And who is the prime example of using power to elevate and honor others? King Jesus himself, which is why Paul grounds all of our relationships at home "in the Lord [Jesus]." Every area of life, and most especially the most intimate ones, must come under the authority of our King, who teaches us how to love sacrificially for the good of others.

This text in Colossians needs to be read with the much longer companion text in Ephesians 5. In Ephesians 5:21, Paul lays the groundwork for his household code by telling us to "submit to one another out of reverence for Christ." Colossians uses a shorthand way to describe this mutual submission: "in the Lord" and "do it all in the name of the Lord Jesus." The rules of the Christian home are not based on hierarchy or even "shared power." Power, hierarchy, and authority are not the focus at all; the sacrificial love of Jesus is. "Wives serve husbands and husbands sacrifice themselves for their wives because that is what love means. Superiority, power, and status

---

[2]Aristotle, *Politics* 1.5.
[3]McKnight, 337.

have all been eradicated in Christoformity…Christoformity bids farewell to hierarchy."[4] Again, McKnight gets it right: "The more emphasis given to love, the more Spirit-driven will be the relationship of husband and wife. The text, then, does not advocate sharing power; it advocates sharing life and love with one another as a new kind of power."[5] With the foundation of King Jesus, let's look at what Paul and Timothy say to wives and husbands.

A Word to Wives. In Greek and Roman society, wives had no choice but to submit to their husbands. While husbands could be sexually promiscuous and divorce their wives at will, wives were dependent on their husbands economically, and society required wives to be submissive to their husbands in every way. But Paul tells wives not to think about their husbands the way the world does. He tells them to "choose" to submit, using the middle passive, indicating she is the one to make that decision. She chooses to submit not because society tells her to, but because she has chosen a different way of life and a different Lord who will take care of her. Her "Lord" is not her husband; her Lord is her Protector, King Jesus. "Instead of grounding the instruction to the wife in her husband's authority, power, leadership, or status in a hierarchy, the grounding is radically otherwise; it is grounded in the Lord's way of life."[6] Wives choose to submit to their husbands in a relationship of mutual submission. This certainly includes loving her husband and thinking about and finding ways that he feels loved. In Ephesians 5:33, Paul emphasizes an important way that husbands feel loved—when they feel *respected.* A wife's admiration and respect are like jet fuel to a husband; conversely, criticism can deaden his soul. The love that a wife shows her husband by respecting and

---

[4]McKnight, 344, 347.
[5]McKnight, 350.
[6]McKnight, 346.

admiring him is a channel for the Spirit-filled love of God to breathe new life into a home.

A Word to Husbands. Because the Christian home is "in the Lord," Paul's word to husbands is also striking. He does not tell them to "lead," he tells husbands to *love*. In Ephesians, Paul says husbands are to love their wives *just like Christ loves us*. In Ephesians, Paul describes how husbands should love their wives by using the term "head." As Christ is the "head of the church," husbands should love their wives as a head does its body. It is unfortunate that when we read that term "head," we immediately interpret it using our Western, English language mindset and translate head to mean "leader." We should instead remember that words used in the Bible need to be interpreted within their context, and this is particularly true of the word "head" (*kephale*). In Ephesians 5:22-33, Paul uses the term "head" to describe how a head "feeds, nourishes, and cares for" a body. Paul had used the term "head" in Eph. 4:15, 16 to describe how we all, as the body of Christ, grow up into maturity in Christ as we are built up in *love*. Paul carries this same thought forward in Eph. 5:22 ff by describing the function of the head as *loving* the body by nourishing, feeding, and caring for it. That is what it means for Christ to be the "head" of the body, and that is what Paul means in Eph. 5:22ff when he says the husband is the head of the wife. Paul is challenging us as husbands not to "lead" our wives, but to *love them*. "It needs to be noted that the husband is not instructed to lead his wife, but to love her sacrificially."[7]

We are to love our wives just as King Jesus has loved us. That means to be committed to her best interests. It means to spend time with her and, when we are with our wives, to be completely focused on her—to listen intently. It means to pro-

---

[7]McKnight, 349.

vide for her, to pray for her continually, to be thinking about her needs and what is best for her. It means praying and working for an environment at home where love is the rule of the house, where everyone feels honored and safe, and where everyone flourishes.

In addressing husbands, Paul uses a term which the NIV translates "don't be harsh" but which could be translated "don't be embittered." Interestingly, Paul tells husbands not to *resent* their wives. Why would he say that? As Wright notes, we husbands

> …must scrupulously avoid the temptation to resent her being the person she is, to become bitter or angry when she turns out to be, like him, a real human being, and not merely the projection of his own hopes or fantasies.[8]

God created men and women for each other. Both are created in God's image, and both can be "recreated" in the image, love, and energy of King Jesus. God said the marriage relationship is "very good" (Gen. 1:31). Unfortunately, our marriages are under attack by all the forces of our culture, including our anxiety driven, fast-paced way of life. But God, the Creator of marriage, can heal, nourish, energize, and restore our marriages. If you are married, commit your whole heart to your spouse, trusting in King Jesus, and let his love and Spirit be the foundation and the rule of your house.

†

Creator God, thank you that in creating us, you created us to be with other people. Thank you for your church, the family where all of us, married or single, can con-

[8]Wright, *Colossians*, 152.

nect on the deepest of spiritual levels. For those of us who are married, we thank you for its blessings, but we acknowledge its serious responsibilities. I commit myself in covenant love to my spouse today, just as you committed yourself completely to me in covenant love in the Incarnation and in the cross. [For husbands: King Jesus, fill me today with your love so that I in turn may serve my wife, imitating how you serve and love me. Help me to listen to her today; help me notice the ways she needs my love and help today. Help me to encourage her and to tell her how much she means to me.] [For wives: King Jesus, fill me today with your love so that I in turn may serve my husband, imitating how you serve and love me. Help me to listen to him today. Help me to let him know how much I respect him, appreciate all he does, and am proud of him.] Lord Jesus, may we be a model of you to a world that doesn't know how to love. Thank you for teaching us what love is.

CHILDREN AND FATHERS

Children, obey your parents in everything, for this pleases the Lord.21 Fathers, do not embitter your children, or they will become discouraged. (3:20, 21)

Children, obey your parents in the Lord, for this is right. 2 "Honor your father and mother"—which is the first commandment with a promise— 3 "so that it may go well with you and that you may enjoy long life on the earth." Fathers, do not exasperate your children; instead, bring them up in the training and instruction of the Lord. (Eph. 6:1-4)

Paul and Timothy continue their "Christ-subverted" discussion of household codes by addressing children and fathers. While children are instructed to obey their "parents," it is noticeable that Paul then gives instruction not to both parents (mothers and fathers), but only to "fathers," both here and in Ephesians. This is probably because the father had particular rights and responsibilities in Roman culture for their children and families. But the emphasis on fathers here is also particularly relevant to our own culture, which is experiencing a crisis in fatherhood. According to the U.S. Census Bureau, 18.4 million children in the U.S. (1 in 4) live without a biological, step, or adoptive father. When a child is raised in a home without a father, they have a 4 times greater risk of living in poverty, are 7 times more likely to become pregnant as a teen, are more likely to abuse drugs and alcohol, and have a greater chance of going to prison.[1] Children from single-parent families are twice as likely to suffer from mental health and behavioral problems as those living with married parents.[2] Conversely, in numerous studies, positive father involvement is associated with children's higher academic achievement; greater school readiness; stronger math and verbal skills; greater emotional security; higher self-esteem; fewer behavioral problems; and greater social competence than found among children who do not have caring, involved fathers.[3] Dads, if you are reading this, your kids are blessed because you are making a commitment to the future of your children and grandchildren.

So what does Paul and Timothy have to say to children and parents (and especially to Dads)?

A Word to Children. When God gave the Torah to the people of Israel, he dignified children by including them in those who should listen to the reading of the Word of the Lord (see Deut. 29:10). Paul and Timothy instruct children to obey their parents "in everything," because "this pleases the Lord [Jesus]." By saying children should obey "in everything," they are not saying that a child must obey a parent if the parent asks them to do something immoral, unethical, or illegal (see, for example, Acts 5:29). But children have a way of conveniently ignoring or not obeying their parents when they don't want to. But obedience

---

[1]U.S. Census Bureau (2021), cited in https://fatherhood.org/new-father-facts-8/.

[2]See https://americafirstpolicy.com/latest/issue-brief-fatherlessness-and-its-effects-on-american-society.

[3]See E. Flouri and A. Buchanan, "The Role of Father Involvement in Children's Later Mental Health," *Journal of Adolescence* 26(2003): 63–78; J. Mosley and E. Thomson, "Fathering Behavior and Child Outcomes: The Role of Race and Poverty," in W. Marsiglio (Ed.) *Research on Men and Masculinities Series 7, Fatherhood: Contemporary Theory, Research and Social Policy* (148–165).

and discipline while a child is still at home have such profound, life-long blessings. Parents really do know better because of their experience and wisdom, and often by ignoring their parents' instructions, children (especially teens) can make tragic, life-altering mistakes. Learning to obey your parents also trains your character to trust and obey our Father, who really does know what is best for us. Maybe that is why in Eph. 6:2,3 Paul, quoting Deut. 5:16, says that honoring our parents is the first commandment "with a promise," and the promise is to us: that we may live long, flourishing lives.

A Word to Fathers. Fathers are not instructed to "lead" or exercise authority. Instead, we are instructed to "nurture" our children. It is interesting how the instruction focuses on not doing something that will harm our children, both in Colossians and in Ephesians: "Don't *embitter* your children, or *they will become discouraged*;" "Don't *exasperate* your children, but bring them up in the training and instruction of the Lord [Jesus]." The word for embitter (*erethizo*) could also be translated "provoke" or "pick a fight," which would "discourage" (*athymeo*) or deflate a child. The emphasis here is on the profound effect a Dad and his words have on children, both negative and positive. As McKnight notes

> …the observation is stunningly modern: the father who berates and embitters a child flattens that child's maturation and converts the child into anger.[4]

A Word to Parents. Parents, our words have a tremendous impact on our children. We have a duty before God to "train" and "instruct" our children in the Lord Jesus, and we should do that as part of our natural, every day way of life (Deut. 6:6). So we pray and talk about what God is doing in our own lives when

[4]McKnight, 355.

we rise up in the morning (communicating to them before work and school); when we walk along the way (when driving to school or other activities); when we eat (the dinner table is the best place); and when we lie down (when we read and pray with them at the end of the day). When a child sees that God is real in her Mom's and Dad's lives, God in turn becomes real to the child, and the Spirit then has access to help our children flourish in life. We would also do well to remember that the best instruction is always preceded by encouragement and then reaffirmed by encouragement. The sequence is: encourage first, then instruct/train, and then encourage again.

Kids today are living in an especially anxious time. Parents can calm that anxiety and give children a safe place of assurance, love, confidence, and peace because of the authority and love of King Jesus in the hearts of Moms and Dads. Let me quote Wright at length on the beauty of a home being "in King Jesus:"

> The parents' duty is, in effect, to live out the gospel to the child: that is, to assure their children that they are loved and accepted and valued for who they are, not what they ought to be, should have been, or might (if only they would try a little harder) become. Obedience must never be made the condition of parental 'love'; a 'love' so conditioned would not deserve the name. When the parent is obedient to the vocation of genuine love, the child's obedience may become, like that of the Christian to God, a glad and loving response.[5]

---

[5]Wright, *Colossians,* 153.

†

Father God, thank you that we learn what parenting is, what "Fatherhood" is, from getting to know you. Thank you so much, Father God, for the wonderful blessings of children. Children teach us so much about life, about ourselves, about you. Today, calm the hectic pace of our lives and our families by gathering us as a family around the dinner table. May our children see that you are real, God, as I let you be real in my life. Thank you that you walk with me through this crazy, fast-paced life, and you slow me down to trust in you. And as I do that, my kids see you and their anxious lives are calmed, too. Thank you, Father God!

A NEW ATTITUDE ABOUT WORK

Slaves, obey your earthly masters in everything, and do it, not only when their eye is on you and to curry their favor, but with sincerity of heart and reverence for the Lord. 23 Whatever you do, work at it with all your heart, as working for the Lord, not for human masters, 24 since you know that you will receive an inheritance from the Lord as a reward. It is the Lord Christ you are serving. 25 Anyone who does wrong will be repaid for their wrongs, and there is no favoritism. (3:22-25)

Masters, provide your slaves with what is right and fair because you know that you also have a Master in heaven. (4:1)

Paul and Timothy devote an extended amount of time to addressing the relationship between slaves and their "masters." This may be because Roman slavery was such an everyday thing in Roman culture. In the first century, there were as many as 60 million slaves in Roman occupied territories. Slaves were initially the people the Romans conquered. As the Roman Empire grew, so did slavery. The Romans (and Greeks) thought work was beneath a free person. The Romans believed the pagan gods created humans to do work, and so the conquering Romans let the slaves do all the work. This work not only included manual labor, but slaves were also doctors, lawyers, teachers, musicians, and other professionals.

Thus, churches were filled with people who were slaves, and often slaves were elders and leaders in the churches (even churches where the master and slaves worshipped together). King Jesus turned all relationships upside down because in the church, there was no distinction between slave and free. Christianity brought dignity and worth to every human being. Although during these first few centuries, Christians did not try to abolish slavery politically (because to do so would have been quickly squelched by the Romans), the leaven of King Jesus was changing how people viewed others and even slavery. And so, Paul could write to his friend Philemon, living in Colossae, who was the master of the runaway slave Onesimus, telling Philemon to welcome Onesimus back "no longer as a slave, but better than a slave, as a dear brother" (Philemon 16). You might want to read the short letter to Philemon today, and when you do, notice the pressure Paul puts on Philemon to, as a Christian, release Onesimus from slavery. Paul makes his appeal "on the basis of love," confident that Philemon will "do even more than I ask" (8, 21). Paul, who had the mind of Christ, would say that "the one who was a slave when called to faith in the Lord is the Lord's freed person; similarly, the one who was free when called is Christ's slave. You were bought at a price; do not become slaves of human beings" (1 Cor. 7:22, 23). Thank God that Christianity did eventually end slavery in the Roman culture, as well as finally put an end to the horrendous slavery in England and America.[1] Before we consider how this passage might have application for us today, we should remind our-

[1]See Alvin J. Schmidt, *Under the Influence: How Christianity Transformed Civilization* (Grand Rapids, MI: Zondervan, 2001), 278.

selves of how prevalent human trafficking still is in our world today and do all that we can to help eradicate it.[2]

How can we apply Paul's and Timothy's instructions to our daily lives? Maybe the closest parallel today is the relationship between employer and employee. How can we apply this passage to our work situation?

Work is a good thing; part of being human means to work. The Greeks and Romans believed the gods created humans to do their work, and that work was a curse. Christianity and Judaism completely changed that way of thinking. God himself is a worker, a Creator, and God still works to this day (John 5:17). Work is not a curse, it is a blessing for our own benefit. Before the Fall, God told the man and the woman to have dominion over and exercise great care for the earth, to subdue and cultivate it. Since we are made in the image of God, and since God creates and works, part of being human is to work and create. "Our potential for creative work is an essential part of our God-like humanness."[3] Christianity brought a completely new and refreshing attitude toward work. Although the curse certainly makes work more difficult at times, King Jesus is in the process of reversing the curse in all aspects of our life, even our work. Paul and Timothy next mention some of the ways that King Jesus reverses the curses in our work by reshaping our attitudes about our work.

Employees, you are not just working for your employer, you are first of all working for the Lord. The first change in attitude about work is a change in who we are working *for*. Although we may be employed by a particular company, we work for the

---

[2]Some good resources in this regard are: Faith Alliance Against Slavery and Trafficking, https://faastinternational.org/about-us/our-mission; Our Daughters International, https://faastinternational.org/about-us/our-mission.

[3]John Stott, "Reclaiming the Biblical Doctrine of Work," *Christianity Today*, May 4, 1979, 36.

Lord Jesus, and that means we know that he will always take care of us. That also means that we don't work just for the sake of work. Living just to receive a paycheck or for the applause of others is a dead end and fails to energize our lives. In King Jesus, we see how work is just one aspect of our larger lives, and our larger lives are about impacting and loving others. When we have that attitude, work becomes a "calling," a vocation. We want to do good work because we want to serve others, and we want to provide good things for our families. That means whatever work we do can bring glory to God. Paul is a great example: Paul's occupation was not preaching, it was tent-making, and Paul viewed both his preaching and his tent-making as ways to serve others. Since we spend most of our time at work, that is the perfect place to glorify God. "Christians should do their work in a distinctively different way, characterized by generosity as opposed to ruthlessness, care for their coworkers and commitment to helping them as opposed to seeking to climb over them, and genuinely serving others as opposed to taking advantage of them."[4]

Our reward in life doesn't just come from our work. Shockingly, Paul tells the slaves of his day that they will "receive an inheritance from the Lord as their reward." This is shocking because slaves had no inheritance rights. But Paul is reminding them that the firstborn Son (who had all the inheritance rights) has given up his rights and given us all the inheritance of becoming sons and daughters, no longer slaves to anything in this life, including being a "slave to work." Unfortunately, we live in a "total work" environment in the U.S., where people are either always texting about work, thinking about work, or promoting themselves on social media for work. We can become frantic and anxious about work when work either becomes our

[4]Hammett and McCoy, *Humanity*, 211.

"idol" or, out of fear, we let work become our master instead of our real Master.

Practice Sabbath. Reminding ourselves where our real rewards in this life come from can help us break free from the slave-hold of work. And one critical way to break free is to practice the God-given gift of *Sabbath.* At least one time a week, we need to STOP (the Hebrew word *Shavat* means "stop" or "cease"). We need to turn over all responsibilities and burdens to God and unplug. God not only gave us an example of being a worker, he also gave us an example of a "rester." "Sabbath rest reminds us that God is the source of all we have. We rest not only to be renewed, but to renew our trust in him as our Provider. The Sabbath also reminds us that God made work for humanity, but did not make humanity for the sole purpose of work; our work finds a right perspective when we rest. Further, humanity images God in rest as well as in work."[5] As Walter Brueggemann writes, "God is not a workaholic. God is not a Pharoah. God does not keep jacking up production schedules. To the contrary, God rests, confident, serene, at peace. God's rest, moreover, bestows on creatureliness a restfulness that contradicts the 'drivenness' of the system of Pharoah."[6]

Employers, treat your employees fair and right because it is not your profit margin to which you will have to answer. Paul's word to "masters" (i.e., employers) is practical and financial:

---

[5]Hammett and McCoy, *Humanity*, 234-35. Some good resources to help you practice Sabbath are: Mark Buchanan, *The Rest of God: Restoring Your Soul by Restoring Sabbath* (Nashville: Thomas Nelson, 2006); Alan Fadling, *An Unhurried Life: Following Jesus' Rhythms of Work and Rest* (Downers Grove, Il: IVP Books, 2013); Jay Y. Kim, *Analog Christian: Cultivating Contentment, Resilience, and Wisdom in the Digital Age* (Downers Grove, Il: IVP, 2022).

[6]Walter Brueggemann, *Sabbath as Resistance: Saying NO to the CULTURE OF NOW* (Louisville, KY: Westminster John Knox Press, 2014), 29, 31.

provide what is right and fair because your "Master" is not the dollar or your profit margin. Your Master is God Almighty, and all of us will have to answer to him for the way we treat others. For employers, that means providing a good wage, good benefits, and a good and healthy working environment. Employers (and any employee who is in a supervisory role) have a tremendous opportunity to help others see and come to King Jesus by the way they treat their employees and subordinates. Perhaps one of the best examples of such an employer in our day is Chick-fil-A. In *It's My Pleasure: The Impact of Extraordinary Talent and Compelling Culture*, Dee Ann Turner chronicles the huge impact Chick-fil-A has had on millions of lives by creating a culture that values people above everything else.[7] The result of putting people first has been a huge business success for the company. But business success is not why Chick-fil-A has the culture that it has. If money was the motivating factor, Chick-fil-A wouldn't be closed every Sunday to give their employees time off. Go online and look at Chick-fil-A's purpose, culture, and values on their website.[8] Their purpose says it all: "To glorify God by being a faithful steward of all that is entrusted to us. To have a positive influence on all who come in contact with Chick-fil-A."

†

Creator God, thank you for work--for letting me also create new things, to be diligent and enjoy the fruit of my work. Thank you also, Creator God, that you have woven rest into creation itself. Forgive me for thinking the outcomes of my work are all up to me. Train me

---

[7]Dee Ann Turner, *It's My Pleasure: The Impact of Extraordinary Talent and Compelling Culture*, (Boise, ID: Elevate Publishing, 2015).
[8]https://www.chick-fil-a.com/.

through Sabbath to realize that you bless those who trust in you. You are not a workaholic, and you do not call me to be a workaholic either, but you call me to rest in you. Let me make Sabbath and worship the center from which your blessings over my work will flow. I love you!

WALKING HABIT: STOP! (PRACTICE SABBATH)

One of the most important practices we can do in our frenetic, anxious world is to *"Stop!" Stop* at least once a week and practice Sabbath. God *commanded* that we keep the Sabbath (the 4th commandment). The Sabbath commandment, just like the rest of the 10 commandments, still stands. Sabbath rest is not just a commandment; God wove it into the very fabric of creation. Christians adopted Sunday, the day of Jesus' resurrection, as the new Sabbath, but it is still required Sabbath rest. Just like all of God's good commandments, Sabbath was given to us by God for our own good: "Sabbath was made for humanity" (Mark 2:27). So be intentional in totally unplugging at least one day per week. Sabbath not only restores our bodies and souls, but it also becomes the center of peace out of which God's blessings will flow.

FULL OF GRACE, SEASONED WITH SALT

Devote yourselves to prayer, being watchful and thankful. 3 And pray for us, too, that God may open a door for our message so that we may proclaim the mystery of Christ, for which I am in chains. 4 Pray that I may proclaim it clearly, as I should. 5 Be wise in the way you act toward outsiders; make the most of every opportunity. 6 Let your conversation be always full of grace, seasoned with salt so that you may know how to answer everyone. (4:2-6)

And pray in the Spirit on all occasions with all kinds of prayers and requests. With this in mind, be alert and always keep on praying for all the Lord's people. 19 Pray also for me, that whenever I speak, words may be given me so that I will fearlessly make known the mystery of the gospel, 20 for which I am an ambassador in chains. Pray that I may declare it fearlessly, as I should. (Eph. 6:18-20)

Paul and Timothy are about to finish their letter, with the last section being personal greetings from and to dear friends. But before they get there, they want to emphasize two important practices that are related to each other: prayer and "gracing" others with the Good News about King Jesus (notice the almost identical passage in Ephesians). We would be wise to remember how connected prayer and concern for others should and can be in our daily lives.

Be Devoted to Praying. A literal translation of the Greek text would be "Prayer—devote yourselves to it."[1] Being "devoted" to prayer means we make it our first priority: in the morning before we begin our day, all during the day when stressful situations occur, and at night when we think back on all the events of the day. Unlike anything else, spending time with God shapes our character and heart, molding us to trust in the God who makes himself real in our lives. Paul expounds in Ephesians by saying that we should pray in the Spirit "on all occasions with all kinds of prayers and requests." That means our first reaction to everything should be taking it to the Lord in prayer. When we pray, we should be "watchful" and "alert." As the Psalmist says, we lay our requests before the Lord in the morning and then wait in expectation (Ps. 5:3). When we pray, we should expect God to listen and to answer us in one way or another. That is one reason keeping a Gratitude journal is such a good practice because often God will answer our prayers in ways we don't expect. Paul and Timothy again mention being thankful (as they have throughout Colossians). We should be expectant, alert to notice God working in our lives, and then full of joy and thanksgiving because we do see God actively working in all of our life situations.

What You Say and Post Should be Full of Grace and Seasoned with Wisdom. Paul and Timothy ask the Colossians to pray for them that they may proclaim the "mystery" that is King Jesus, and that they may do it "clearly" (and in Ephesians, "fearlessly"). Paul has talked a lot about the Christian

---

[1]Thompson, 97.

faith being a "mystery" that God kept hidden in the past but that now is proclaimed all over the world to Gentiles and Jews alike. In many ways, the Christian faith is a mystery—that the great God of the universe became a human; that the way to rescue humans is through suffering and a cross; that death is not the end because Jesus rose from the dead; and all authority has been given to King Jesus, who is transforming the world not by power but by grace and truth. All these mysteries answer the human dilemma of understanding God, overcoming our selfish tendencies, dealing with suffering, and overcoming our fear of death. It is important that we as Christians let the mysteries of King Jesus dwell in us through letting the Word of God permeate our minds and character. Then we will be able to know how to answer people who ask us why our lives are so different. We don't have to be prepared to provide complex theological answers. That's not what people usually want anyway; what they want is to know why *we* believe. As Peter said, we just tell them why we believe; we tell them our own reason for the hope that we have (1 Peter 3:15). Peter goes on to say that we should do that "with gentleness and respect" (1 Pet. 3:15). Paul similarly says that our speech (and we could say, our social media posts) should be "*full* of grace, seasoned with salt." Whenever we talk to people (or whatever we post), people should come away thinking that we are gracious people, kind, considerate, forgiving, and patient (Col. 3:12). They may disagree with us, but they should feel sorry for disagreeing with us because they like us so much! People are usually not won over by logical arguments (although in due time they may become hungry to learn more about the Christian faith). They are usually won over when they realize that we really care for them. People don't care how much you know until they know how much you care.

So what does it mean that our speech should be "seasoned with salt"? Salt was used to bring flavor and to preserve. In the same way, our speech should not repel people but should instead intrigue them. Salty speech is "gracious, wise, informed, and redemptive speech."[2] That type of speech will be a natural outgrowth of a life that lets the Word of Christ dwell richly, and a life whose character has been shaped over the long haul by prayer. That type of speech also comes about by the working of God, who opens opportunities for us when we are "watchful," and who himself goes before us to prepare the hearts of those we pray for and interact with. As Jesus said, "Don't worry about what to say or how to say it. At that time, you will be given what to say, for it will not be you speaking but the Spirit of your Father speaking through you" (Matt. 10:19, 20).

†

Father God, I praise you that you invite me into a quiet place to talk with you, and you, the Creator God of the whole universe, listen to me! You listen to me because you care for me! You want me to listen to you, too, so open my ears and heart to hear what you want to say to me. Speak through your Word, through others, and in the quietness of our time together. I will not be anxious about anything, but in turning it over to you by prayer and requests, you will fill me with a peace that is beyond understanding. Thank you for being the "With Me" God.

[2]McKnight, 380.

WALKING HABIT: PRAYER—DEVOTE YOURSELF TO IT

Fittingly, our last "Walking Habit" is prayer. Paul and Timothy tell us to be "devoted to prayer," which means prayer needs to be intentional, and we need to work at it. Being devoted to prayer means we pursue it until the "duty becomes a delight."[3] Prayer should be a bookend to each of our days (morning and evening), and should fill the middle of each day (remembering to pray in stressful situations or to give thanks). Morning and evening prayer might follow the "outline" Jesus gave us in the Lord's Prayer:

- *A time of adoration and praise*. Think about Who you are talking to. Invite him into your presence. Prepare your mind by meditating on a Psalm or the character of God. Remember all God has done for you and give thanks. Open your hands and invite God in.
- *Examine your heart*. Ask God to reveal your heart to you. Confess your failings, your fears, your anger—pour it all out to God. Ask for forgiveness; forgive others who have hurt you. Ask God to bring the warmth of his love and forgiveness so you can actually feel his love.
- *Pour out all your requests to God*. Bring before him your needs and people in your life. Instead of a "list" of people and needs, ask God to help you know how to pray for them and how you might help them.
- *End with adoration and praise*. Reciting Psalm 23 is a beautiful way to end your time with the Good Shepherd.

---

[3]See J.I. Packer and Carolyn Nystrom, *Praying: Finding Our Way through Duty to Delight* (Downers Grove, Il: InterVarsity Press, 2009).

LET THE REVOLUTION BEGIN

Tychicus will tell you all the news about me. He is a
dear brother, a faithful minister and fellow servant in
the Lord. 8 I am sending him to you for the express
purpose that you may know about our circumstances
and that he may encourage your hearts. 9 He is coming
with Onesimus, our faithful and dear brother, who is
one of you. They will tell you everything that is happen-
ing here. My fellow prisoner Aristarchus sends you his
greetings, as does Mark, the cousin of Barnabas. (You
have received instructions about him; if he comes to
you, welcome him.) 11 Jesus, who is called Justus, also
sends greetings. These are the only Jews among my co-
workers for the kingdom of God, and they have proved
a comfort to me. 12 Epaphras, who is one of you and a
servant of Christ Jesus, sends greetings. He is always
wrestling in prayer for you, that you may stand firm in
all the will of God, mature and fully assured. 13 I vouch
for him that he is working hard for you and for those at
Laodicea and Hierapolis. 14 Our dear friend Luke, the
doctor, and Demas send greetings. 15 Give my greet-
ings to the brothers and sisters at Laodicea, and to
Nympha and the church in her house. 16 After this let-
ter has been read to you, see that it is also read in the
church of the Laodiceans and that you in turn read the

> *letter from Laodicea. Tell Archippus: "See to it that you complete the ministry you have received in the Lord." I, Paul, write this greeting in my own hand. Remember my chains. Grace be with you. (4:7-16)*

Paul and Timothy are huddled together in chains in a prison cell, either in Ephesus or Rome. They are in prison because they have been preaching about some Jewish guy named Jesus, whom they claim is the human manifestation of God himself. It is shocking that Paul would believe this because of Paul's pristine Jewish orthodoxy. Yet Paul was completely convinced because this Jesus actually did rise from the dead, appearing to not only over 500 people but to Paul, too (1 Cor. 15:6). Paul would tell you that God himself convinced Paul that this was God's mysterious plan all along. The plan was that God loved the humans he created so much that even before he created them, he had intended to recreate them in love. God had intended to rescue us by coming to us, reaching out to us, reconciling us to him, and recreating us to become the humans he had created us to be in the first place. And this Jesus--this selfless, humble, authentic, sacrificial, powerful, loving, resurrected Jesus--was and is the prototype, the blueprint, for humanity. Jesus had begun a revolution, and it had spread like wildfire, starting in Jerusalem, then to all of Judea, Samaria, and Syria, and now having reached the Asian towns of Colossae, Ephesus, Laodicea, and Hierapolis, and then on to Athens, Corinth, Rome, and to the ends of the world.

And so Paul and Timothy write this letter to a church in Colossae they have never been to. But in these last few verses we see the close bonds, the new family ties, that Christianity was creating all over the Roman Empire. In prison with Paul is Aristarchus and Mark, Barnabas' cousin. You remember Mark. Many years before, young Mark was traveling with Paul and

Barnabas, but then he got homesick and had to go back to Jerusalem (Acts 15:36ff). At first, Paul didn't want to trust Mark again. And yet, because of how much King Jesus had changed Paul, Mark and Paul were reconciled, and Paul says that if Mark comes to Colossae, they should welcome him. [By the way, Mark went on to write the Gospel of Mark]. Others with Paul are Dr. Luke (a Gentile convert to Christianity who also wrote a Gospel), Jesus Justus, Demas, and Epaphras, a native of Colossae who was the first to tell the Colossians about Jesus.

Paul and Timothy are sending their letter with two men: Tychicus (who was also the one that brought the circular letter of Ephesians), and Onesimus, the runaway slave who is now a brother in Christ. Paul is probably also sending a letter with Onesimus to Philemon, with the appeal that Philemon welcome him back not as a slave, but now as a freed brother in the Lord. Paul specifically mentions Philemon's son, Archippus (Philemon 2), in this final greeting, with the admonition that Paul would tell all of us: "See to it that you complete the ministry you have received in the Lord."

The church in Colossae probably met in the house of Philemon (Philemon 2). The house church just down the road in Laodicea met in the home of a woman named Nympha. Paul had written a letter to the Laodicean church, too, and he tells the Colossians to make sure they let the church in Nympha's house read the Colossian letter and that they, in turn, read the one he wrote to the Laodicean Christians. Unfortunately, we have lost that letter Paul wrote to the Laodiceans. Or have we? Could that letter be the one we now call Ephesians, particularly since Ephesians and Colossians are so similar? We won't know for sure, but what we do know is that these two letters set the world on fire at a very dark time in world history. And the blaze continued to spread and transform cultures the world over. That blaze is the Love of God in Jesus Christ that transforms us into humans in a very dehumanizing world.

As Dallas Willard wrote, Jesus started a "perpetual world revolution:"

> One that is still in process and will continue until God's will is done on earth as it is in heaven. As this revolution culminates, all the forces of evil known to mankind will be defeated and the goodness of God will be known, accepted, and joyously conformed to in every aspect of human life. He has chosen to accomplish this with and, in part, through his students. The revolution of Jesus is in the first place and continuously a revolution of the human heart and spirit…His is a revolution of character, which proceeds by changing people from the inside through ongoing personal relationship to God in Christ and to one another. It is one that changes their ideas, beliefs, feelings, and habits of choice, as well as their bodily tendencies and social relations. It penetrates to the deepest layers of their soul. Churches would naturally be the result. Churches are not the kingdom of God, but are primary and inevitable expressions, outposts, and instrumentalities of the kingdom among us. They are 'societies' of Jesus… as the reality of Christ is brought to bear on ordinary human life.[1]

†

King Jesus, praise your name for coming to us and for starting a revolution that transformed and continues to transform the world. King Jesus, we believe you are the

---

[1]Willard, *Renovation of the Heart*, 15, 16.

hope for humanity--the hope to rescue us from ourselves and from all the oppressive powers in our lives, from the fear of death, and from death itself. Today, I will remain in you and allow you to remain in me so that I may be transformed into your image from one degree of glory to another. Father God, to you be glory in the church and in King Jesus throughout all generations, for ever and ever! Amen!

DISCUSSION QUESTIONS

Colossians 1:1,2

1. Who wrote the letter to the Colossians, and what was their background? How do you think they became Christians?
2. Why do you think Paul said he was an apostle of King Jesus "by the will of God"? Do you think God has a "will" for your life, and what is it?
3. What are some of the traits Paul uses to describe the Christians in Colossae?
4. What does "holy" mean? How do you become holy?
5. What does "faithful" mean? How do you become faithful?
6. Paul frequently uses the phrase "in Christ" throughout Colossians and his other letters. What does it mean to be "in Christ"? How is being "in Christ" related to having Christ "in you"?

Colossians 1:3-6

1. Why do we as Christians have hope? In what ways is hope becoming real *now*, making a difference in your life *now*? How does hope produce faith and love?
2. Why do you think grace and truth are both important? The Gospel of John says, "grace and truth came through Jesus Christ" (Jn. 1:17). How does Jesus bring both grace and truth? How does God's grace and truth work together in your life?
3. According to our secular culture, what is "truth?" Are there any absolute truths?

4. Secular culture prizes values such as love, equality, the dignity and worth of all humans, freedom, and concern for the marginalized. Where did these values originate?
5. The Hebrews understood truth as *personal,* and the Hebrew word for "truth" means "trustworthy." Does this help you believe what the Bible says about how to live? Why?
6. How can we know God is trustworthy and reliable?

Colossians 1:7,8

1. Who first told the Colossian Christians about Jesus? How did they see Jesus in this person's life?
2. Do you agree with this sentence: "Friendship with other Christians is essential to following Jesus"? How can we develop deeper friendships?
3. How is "Christ in you" and the Holy Spirit working in you the same or similar?
4. How does Jesus reveal what God is like?
5. According to Jesus and Paul, what are some things the Spirit does? What does the Spirit's work in your life mean to you?

Colossians 1:9-14

1. Paul prays that God fill the Colossians with knowledge of his will, with all spiritual wisdom and understanding. What is God's will? (See John 6:40 and John 17:3). What does it mean to "know" God according to the Bible?
2. What is spiritual wisdom? How does wisdom help us in life? How do we attain spiritual wisdom?
3. According to Col. 1:10-12, what are some of the reasons why God gives us knowledge of him and spiritual wisdom and understanding?

4. How does God's "Big Will" for our lives help us in making decisions?
5. What questions should we consider when making big decisions in life?
6. How are we raised up with Jesus now? How does "heaven" begin now?
7. Do you agree with the author's view of "Biblical" and "un-Biblical" understandings of heaven? Why or why not?

Colossians 1:14-20

1. What are your impressions after reading 1:14-20? What does this passage claim about Jesus?
2. How is Jesus the image of the invisible God?
3. The Bible also says humans are made in the image of God. What does it mean to say that humans are made in the "image" of God?
4. Paul says Jesus is the "prototype" or blueprint for humans. What does that mean to you?
5. What does it mean to you that all things were created by Jesus? And that all things were created for Jesus? What were God's purposes in creating us?
6. Why do you think Paul brings up the church in the middle of this hymn to Jesus? Is the church important to God? Is the church important to us becoming human again?
7. Paul says Jesus was the "firstborn from the dead." What does that mean for you?
8. Has God already reconciled us to himself? How has he done that? What do we need to do in light of this?

Colossians 1:24-27

1. What do you think Paul means when he says, "I fill up in my flesh what is still lacking in regards to Christ's afflictions for the sake of his body, which is the church"?

2. Does Jesus still suffer and hurt for people (see Acts 9:4; Matt. 25:45)?

3. Do you think Jesus calls us to join him in suffering for people? How might we do that?

4. In what ways does Jesus reveal the mystery that is God?

5. How does Jesus reveal the mystery of all that God planned when he created the universe and humans?

6. In what ways does Jesus answer the mystery of humanity and our destiny?

7. If King Jesus is the mystery of God hidden for ages and generations but now fully revealed to all people, how also is God's mystery "*Christ in you, the hope of glory*?"

8. When Paul says, "Christ in you," is he referring to Christ being in each of us individually or corporately as the church? Or both?

Colossians 1:28-2:6

1. What does Paul say is his goal in writing to the Colossians (1:28, 29)? What does it mean to "mature in Christ"?

2. What are some ways we can mature in Christ?

3. How do you think being in a close-knit community of Jesus followers helps us mature in Christ? What are some practical ways you can bring about such a "close-knit" community?

4. What does it mean to say Jesus is "Lord"? Do you think that is essential to becoming mature in Christ? Why?

5. Paul often uses the term "walk" to describe our maturing in Christ (see also Psalm 1). What does it look like to "walk" in Jesus?

6. What does it mean to be "rooted and built up" in Jesus? How is this related to being "built up in his love" (Eph. 3:17)?

7. Do you think being thankful helps us become more joyful and content? Why?

Colossians 2:4-10, 16-23

1. What were some of the things the "philosophy" in Colossae was teaching?

2. Verses 16-23 indicates that the false teachers were claiming that acceptance by God and heightened spiritual experiences come from participating in Jewish ceremonial practices. Can you see how the Jews would think that? How has Jesus changed this?

3. The false teachers (and Greek philosophy) taught that the body was not important, only the spirit or soul. Do you think our bodies are important? What does the Bible say about our bodies? (1 Cor. 6:12-20; 1 Tim. 4:4).

4. Do you think our secular culture today also separates our bodies from our “feelings” or “person”? In what ways does *dualism* impact how people view sex, abortion, and gender?

Colossians 2:11-15

1. What was circumcision a “sign” of? (see Gen. 17:9-14) How was circumcision a foreshadowing of the “reality” now found in Jesus?

2. What is “circumcision of the heart”? (see Deut. 10:16; Rom. 2:28, 29)

3. How does Jesus now bring about both what circumcision signified and “circumcision of the heart”?

4. In Col. 2:12, Paul compares baptism to circumcision. Why do you think God gave us the gift of baptism? What are some of the “pictures” that baptism paints for us?

5. In Col. 2:13-14, Paul says that God erased all our failures (the “scorecard” against us), nailing it into Jesus on the cross. What does that mean to you? How does the cross “disarm” all the powers that are against you?

6. What illustration does Paul use to describe how Jesus made a “public spectacle” of the powers of shame, fear, worry, regret, bitterness, and anger? How has Jesus triumphed over all these “powers”?

Colossians 2:20-3:4

1. Why do you think Paul says willpower alone will not change us?

2. What are the various "parts of our human self" (or members of our bodies, as Paul says in Col. 3:5 and Rom. 6:13)?

3. Dallas Willard said, "When the mind is right and the heart is right and the body and the soul and the relationships that we have in our social world are right, the whole person simply steps into the way of Christ and lives there with joy and strength. It is not a struggle." Do you agree?

4. How does "setting our hearts on (seeking) things above, where Christ is" change us? What does it mean to "seek the things above"? How is this related to Jesus telling us to pray that God's will be done on earth as it is being done in heaven? (Matt. 6:10)

5. Why does Jesus say that our heart is where our "treasures" are? How does what we love motivate all that we do? How does Jesus give us a "new love"?

6. How does Jesus give us a "new story?" What is the "Big Story" (metanarrative) of Jesus and how does that impact your "story?"

Colossians 3:2-7

1. What does it mean to "set your minds on things above"? Is Paul calling us to an "other-worldliness" that is not con-

nected to our current lives, or something else? How is this related to Paul's statements in Rom. 12:2 and Rom. 8:5-8?

2. How does the way we think and what we think about shape who we are? Do you agree with Dallas Willard's statement: "Nothing enters the mind without having an effect of good or evil?"

3. What habit do you currently do that allows God to train the way you think about everything? What new habit might help?

4. Paul likens sexual immorality (*porneia*) to greed. Why do you think the Bible makes that connection? What is greed?

5. Why is the "wrath of God" coming on the sexually immoral and greedy? What is the "wrath of God"? Why is the wrath of God part of his love for us?

6. Do you think our habits make us who we are? Do good habits become easier to do? Do bad habits become easier to do? Why?

7. How do we change our habits?

8. What does Paul (and Jesus) tell us we must do to stop any bad habit (especially addictive behaviors)? (See Col. 3:5, Matt. 5:30). Why is confession to another person critical in doing this?

9. How is changing who we are like athletic *training*? Do you agree with Dallas Willard's statement: "To train means arranging our life around those practices that enable us to do what we cannot now do by direct effort"? So how do we

allow God to *train* us spiritually to become more like Christ?

10. The reading identifies some "soul training" exercises. Which ones do you currently use to train your soul, and what impact have they had on you? Are there any that you intend to start doing? By the way, who is our "coach" (*paraclete*) in this soul training?

Colossians 3:8-17

1. Do you think social media can harden us into "silos" of disagreement? Why is this? What impact do our words and media posts have? How does Jesus change the way we say or post things?

2. How is slandering someone "blasphemy"? How do we blaspheme God if we belittle others, including those that are not Christians?

3. Paul says we should "put off" our old group solidarity and "put on" a new humanity. Where is this new humanity? How is this new humanity different than the world's cultural or political groups?

4. How do we break out of stereotyping other people? In what ways is Jesus still breaking down cultural, ethnic, racial, gender, and even political divisions today?

5. How is hate a "defensive" strategy? Why is hate a horrible way to protect yourself? Why is love the best way to protect yourself?

6. What are some "pieces" of the armor of love? How does each piece change a relationship or situation? How does love completely change the mood in a room?

7. How is love "offensive"? How might love change relationships and life situations? Who is our model in this?

8. How would you define "worship"? Why is worship so important to our souls? What happens when we worship?

Colossians 3:18-21:

1. The Greek "household codes" were based on the supposed "natural superiority" of masters, parents, and husbands. What are Christian "household codes" based on? Who is the prime example of using power to honor and elevate others?

2. In Eph. 5:21, Paul begins his household codes by calling for "mutual submission" out of our love and reverence for Christ. How does "mutual" submission color how a husband loves his wife, and how a wife loves her husband?

3. If you are a wife, think about some practical ways that you can show your husband how much you love and respect him.

4. If you are a husband, think of some practical ways that you can show your wife how much you love and cherish her.

5. In Col. 3:21, Paul tells fathers not to "embitter" or "provoke" their children, or they might become "discouraged." Do you think this is relevant today? Why?

6. What are practical ways that parents might train their children "when you rise up, walk along the path, and lie down" (Deut. 6:7)?

Colossians 3:22-4:6:

1. Is work a good thing? How is work an essential part of our "Godlike humanness"?

2. According to Paul, who are we working for? How does that change the way we view work? Do you pray for God to bless your work?

3. Is God a workaholic? Why do you think God *commanded* the Sabbath? Practically speaking, how can you obey God's command to practice Sabbath?

4. How can you impact the people you work with? How might the way you treat your employees or fellow workers change their lives?

5. What do you think Paul means by saying that our conversation should be "full of grace, seasoned with salt"? How is this related to what Peter says in 1 Peter 3:15 about treating others (and especially non-Christians) with "gentleness and respect"?

6. Paul says we should "devote" ourselves to prayer? Practically, how can you "devote" yourself to prayer?

7. How is being "watchful and thankful" important when we pray?

Colossians 4:7-16

1. Who is Onesimus? Who is Philemon? How is the letter to Philemon related to Colossians? Have you read the letter to Philemon?

2. In reading this passage, what impression do you get about how much the early Christians loved each other? How did this love come about? How did this love change the world?

3. What happened to the letter Paul wrote to the Laodiceans? Do you think we might still have that letter, just called by another name?

4. What are some things that impressed you in reading Colossians? How has Colossians changed the way you view Jesus? The way you view humanity?

5. In what ways does Jesus make us human in an inhuman world?

About the Author

If you feel generous and have a couple of minutes, please leave a review. It makes a huge difference to the author. Thank you in advance.

Robert C. Beasley is a graduate of the Houston Graduate School of Theology (M.A. in Theological Studies, 2003), the University of Texas Law School (J.D., 1986), and Abilene Christian University (B.A., 1983). He is the author of *Meet God (Before You Die), The Judge and the Left-Footed Leaders: Judges and Ruth for Post-Modern Times*, *From Fish to Glory: 1 Peter for Daily Living,* and *Set Me Free! Understanding our Traditions in the Light of Grace.* He practices law in Houston, Texas, and he and his wife, Stacy, have two grown sons.

Visit the author's website at
http://crazygracetalk.com

FaceBook
http://facebook.com/crazygracetalk

About the Publisher

Sulis International Press publishes select fiction and nonfiction in a variety of genres under four imprints:

- Riversong Books (fiction)
- Sulis Press (general nonfiction)
- Keledei Publications (spirituality)
- Sulis Academic Press (academic works)

For more, visit the website at
https://sulisinternational.com

Subscribe to the newsletter at
https://sulisinternational.com/subscribe/

Follow on social media
https://www.facebook.com/SulisInternational
https://twitter.com/Sulis_Intl
https://www.pinterest.com/Sulis_Intl/
https://www.instagram.com/sulis_international/

www.ingramcontent.com/pod-product-compliance
Lightning Source LLC
Chambersburg PA
CBHW030912090426
42737CB00007B/173